MAXMETRICS® PROJECT LEADERSHIP SERIES

The Hidden Stakeholders of Artificial Intelligence

How to Build AI Projects That Don't Harm People

GLORIA J. MILLER, DBA

ATLANTA | HEIDELBERG

The Hidden Stakeholders of Artificial Intelligence

Published by Maxmetrics LLC, Atlanta, Georgia.

Library of Congress Control Number: 2026908030

International Standard Book Number:

978-0-9983484-9-0 Paperback United States

978-0-9983484-8-3 Paperback Europe

979-8-9952095-4-6 e-Pub

979-8-9952095-5-3 Kindle

Dedication

To the people affected by systems they never chose.

Preface

After more than twenty years working on decision support, expert systems, big data, and artificial intelligence projects, I have seen firsthand the influence project teams have in shaping the systems that increasingly guide our lives.

When ChatGPT and similar tools entered public awareness in 2023, the world suddenly began to recognize both the capabilities and the implications of artificial intelligence. Public discussion quickly turned to questions about when AI might surpass human intelligence, or whether such systems could become uncontrollable.

But before we speculate about superhuman machines, it is worth remembering something simpler and more immediate: these systems are built by people, and they are built in projects.

Artificial intelligence is no longer experimental. AI systems now influence hiring decisions, loan approvals, fraud detection, workplace management, and many other aspects of daily life. They can improve efficiency, expand access to services, and even help save lives. At the same time, they can cause serious harm. Often, the individuals and communities most affected by these systems have the least power to influence how they are designed or deployed.

Project teams therefore bear an extraordinary responsibility. The choices made during design, development, and deployment determine what these systems can and cannot do.

This book grew from both my research into accountability in AI projects and my experience managing complex technology initiatives that require meaningful stakeholder engagement. Again and again, I have seen how easily important voices are overlooked and how difficult it can be to identify those who may be affected by automated decisions.

The purpose of this book is to offer a practical approach for identifying those hidden stakeholders and ensuring their interests are considered. It introduces a structured framework that project teams can use to understand stakeholder risks, clarify responsibilities, and build systems that are responsible, transparent, and sustainable.

Project managers and project teams help shape the systems that shape society. The decisions made in project rooms today may influence the lives of individuals and communities for years to come. Recognizing this responsibility does not mean avoiding innovation; it means building systems with foresight, humility, and care.

My hope is that this book encourages project leaders to pause at the right moments—when decisions about data, models, and deployment are still being made—and ask an essential question: who may be affected by this system, and how can we ensure their interests are considered?

If this book helps even a few project teams see those stakeholders more clearly and act on that responsibility, it will have served its purpose.

Gloria J. Miller, DBA

Contents

IV When Things Go Wrong

V Stakeholder Mapping Method and Tools

VI Governance and Oversight

VII Closing and References

List of Figures

List of Tables

Introduction: The Problem No One Owns

Artificial intelligence (AI) is rapidly becoming embedded across industries. It helps organizations analyze large amounts of data, automate decisions, and improve efficiency (OECD, 2019).

In healthcare, AI can help detect disease. In finance, it can identify fraudulent transactions. In logistics, it can optimize routes and schedules.

But AI systems can also cause harm (Wieringa, 2020).

An automated system may unfairly deny someone a job. A facial recognition system may misidentify a person. A scheduling algorithm may push workers into unstable conditions (Chasalow & Levy, 2021).

These harms may continue long after the original project team has moved on.

The difficult truth is this:

> In many AI projects, no one clearly owns responsibility for harm.

Projects end. Teams change roles. Vendors deliver systems to operators. Operators rely on outputs they did not design.

Meanwhile, the individuals affected may not even know that an algorithm influenced the decision (Martin, 2019).

This situation reflects a broader governance problem.

Artificial intelligence systems are rarely built or used by a single actor. They emerge from a chain of decisions made by designers, project managers, executives, operators, and regulators. When responsibility is distributed across many roles, accountability can become difficult to trace.

In many AI projects, governance breaks down not because rules are absent, but because risks and responsibilities are not clearly identified when key decisions are made. The stakeholders most affected by the system are often identified too late to shape those decisions. Oversight mechanisms are often established only after deployment, and intervention tends to follow only once harm has already occurred.

As a result, problems that begin as small technical or operational decisions can accumulate over a system's lifecycle.

By the time the consequences become visible, responsibility may be difficult to assign, and correcting the system may be costly or politically contentious.

Understanding how these governance failures emerge is the first step toward preventing them.

Later chapters examine these governance failures in more detail and show how they recur in AI projects across various industries.

The Missing Stakeholders

Most project plans focus on stakeholders who can influence success:

- Sponsors and executives
- Project managers
- Developers and engineers
- Business users
- Regulators

This approach works when success means delivering scope on time and within budget.

However, AI systems introduce another category of stakeholders.

These are people who may be affected by the system but have little or no influence over the project. In this book, we call them **passive stakeholders**.

They include:

- Customers affected by automated decisions
- Workers managed by algorithms
- Members of the public

- Vulnerable communities
- The environment

> Passive stakeholders are people who may be affected by an AI system but lack the power to influence the project that created it.

These stakeholders are often invisible during early project decisions. Yet they are frequently the people most affected when AI systems fail.

Ignoring them creates ethical, legal, and reputational risk (European Commission, 2016; Martin, 2019).

Many of the governance failures discussed later in this book begin with precisely this problem: the people most affected by the system were never part of the conversation.

The Governance Challenge

Responsible AI governance requires more than technical accuracy or regulatory compliance.

It requires understanding how systems interact with the people and communities they affect.

This means asking questions that many projects overlook:

- Who may be affected by this system?
- Who is responsible if harm occurs?
- Who reviews system impacts after deployment?

- Who has the authority to intervene if problems appear?

Without clear answers to these questions, governance gaps can emerge even in well-intentioned projects.

What This Book Provides

This book introduces a practical method for identifying stakeholders and clarifying responsibility before harm occurs.

It provides tools that help project teams:

- Identify stakeholders who may be affected by AI systems
- Evaluate stakeholder risks using structured tests
- Document responsibility across project roles
- Establish governance practices that remain active throughout the system's lifecycle

The goal is not to slow innovation or prevent organizations from using AI.

It is to ensure that intelligent systems are developed and deployed in ways that recognize the people they may affect.

Because when AI systems influence human lives, responsibility does not disappear.

It must be designed in.

How to Use This Book

This book helps project leaders expand their view of stakeholders and responsibility across the lifecycle of an AI system

This chapter explains how the book is organized and how readers can use the framework and tools presented in later sections.

What You Will Learn

The book introduces three core ideas.

1. AI systems operate as chains of decisions that affect different stakeholder groups.
2. Every AI project involves a small set of recurring stakeholder roles.
3. Project teams can use a practical method to identify stakeholders and clarify responsibility before systems are deployed.

To support this process, the book introduces four simple tests that help teams identify stakeholders who might otherwise be overlooked:

- **Power**: Who can influence the project?

- **Legitimacy**: Who has a valid claim to be considered?
- **Urgency**: Who may require immediate attention?
- **Harm**: Who could be affected if the system causes harm?

These tests help project teams identify stakeholders who may have little influence over the project but who could experience its consequences. The harm test is particularly important: it reveals *passive stakeholders*—individuals and communities affected by a system even though they have no direct power within the project.

How the Book Is Organized

The book is organized into seven parts, moving from understanding the problem to applying practical solutions.

Part I: Understanding AI Projects

This section explains how AI systems work and why their impacts extend beyond traditional project boundaries. It introduces the concept of the AI system chain and shows how decisions made during development can affect stakeholders later.

Part II: Why AI Projects Are Different

These chapters explain how automated systems influence decisions and why their consequences may not become apparent until well after deployment. The section also introduces common failure patterns and the governance gaps that emerge when stakeholder risks are not identified early.

Part III: The Stakeholder Map

This section introduces the six stakeholder roles that appear in every AI project and explains the concept of passive stakeholders. It presents the four tests—power, legitimacy, urgency, and harm—as a practical framework for identifying and classifying those stakeholders.

Part IV: When Things Go Wrong

Real-world case studies illustrate how AI systems can harm stakeholders when responsibility and governance are unclear. These examples show how stakeholder risks emerge across different industries and at different stages of the AI system lifecycle.

Part V: Stakeholder Mapping Method and Tools

This section presents the practical method introduced in the book. It explains the stakeholder responsibility workshop and provides tools that project teams can use to identify stakeholders, assess potential harms, and document responsibility.

Part VI: Governance and Oversight

These chapters show how organizations can translate stakeholder analysis into governance practices. They introduce governance principles and tools that help ensure accountability throughout the lifecycle of an AI system. Together, the stakeholder workshop and governance framework provide a practical approach to closing the governance gaps identified earlier in the book.

Part VII: Closing and References

The final section reflects on the importance of stakeholder responsibility in the age of intelligent systems and provides sources for further study.

A Practical Guide

This book can be read from beginning to end, but it is also designed as a practical reference.

Readers who want to understand the broader context may begin with Parts I–IV. Project teams seeking practical guidance may move directly to the stakeholder workshop and tools in Part V.

> AI projects are not complete when the system is delivered. They are complete only when the risks to all affected stakeholders have been considered.

Part I

Understanding AI Projects

Chapter 1

How AI Projects Work and Why Stakeholders Matter

Artificial intelligence is often described as a single technology. In reality, AI systems are chains of interconnected components that transform data into decisions (OECD, 2019).

Understanding this chain is essential for identifying stakeholders and managing risk across the system's lifecycle.

AI systems function as artificial agents. They receive inputs, process information, and produce outputs that influence decisions and actions (Miller, 2022b).

Some systems operate with human supervision. Others act automatically with little or no direct oversight.

Artificial agency does not imply moral responsibility.

AI systems can perform tasks, but they do not bear ethical or legal accountability. Responsibility remains with the people and organizations that design, deploy, and oversee them (Gibert & Martin, 2022; Heaton et al., 2023).

The AI System Chain

Most AI systems include several connected steps:

1. **Source Data**: Information collected from systems, platforms, sensors, or people
2. **Data Preparation**: Cleaning, labeling, and organizing data
3. **Training Data**: Data used to train machine learning models
4. **Model Development**: Building and validating predictive algorithms
5. **User Interface**: The point where people or systems interact with the AI
6. **Decisions and Consequences**: The real-world outcomes produced by the system

Because each stage involves different activities and decisions, different stakeholders become visible at different points in the system lifecycle.

Data subjects may be affected when information is collected. Developers influence outcomes during model design. Users influence how systems are applied. Decision subjects experience the final consequences.

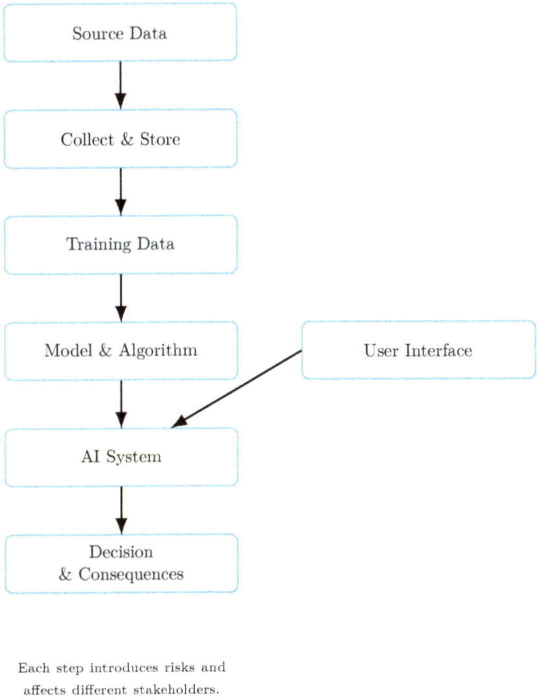

Figure 1.1: The AI System Chain: from data to real-world consequences.

Three Lifecycle Phases

It is useful to view AI projects in three stages (OECD, 2019):

- **Development**: Designing and building the system
- **Usage**: Deploying and operating the system
- **Consequence**: The long-term effects of decisions

Consequences may appear months or years after deployment. That delay often separates decision-makers from accountability (Wieringa, 2020).

Changing Stakeholders Over Time

Different groups hold influence at different stages.

During Development

- Project funders and sponsors
- Project managers
- Data scientists and engineers
- Legal and compliance teams

During Usage

- Operating organizations
- End users
- Platform providers
- Model maintainers

During Consequences

- Decision subjects
- Workers
- Vulnerable groups
- Local communities
- The environment

The people who design an AI system are rarely the ones who experience its consequences. This separation between designers and affected individuals creates a structural responsibility gap. Research confirms that affected communities and end users are frequently underrepresented in AI development compared to technical teams and organizational leaders (Kuehnert et al., 2025).[1] Participatory approaches can reduce these blind spots, but they require time, resources, and institutional support (Heaton et al., 2023).

Understanding this gap is the first step toward responsible AI development.

Emerging Forms of AI

The structure described above applies to all AI systems. However, recent developments have increased both their scale and autonomy.

Generative and General-Purpose AI

Generative AI systems produce text, images, audio, and video. These models are trained on large datasets and generate new content in response to prompts (Zhang et al., 2025).

These technologies are often described as "general-purpose." Their value lies in their broad applicability across industries and workflows (Qin et al., 2025). They can support customer service, software development, content creation, legal drafting, education, and many other tasks.

However, broad utility should not be confused with autonomy. A system may be widely applicable without independently defining its own goals.

Agentic AI and Increasing Autonomy

Agentic AI systems are designed to pursue assigned objectives and execute sequences of tasks with limited human intervention (Nisa et al., 2025). Rather than responding only to direct prompts, such systems may plan actions, adapt to new information, and modify their strategies dynamically (Sapkota et al., 2026).

This increases technical autonomy. However, autonomy does not transfer accountability. Responsibility remains with the developers, operators, and the organizations that deploy these systems (Heaton et al., 2023).

As autonomy grows, so does the importance of clear governance.

Why This Structure Matters

AI projects are not single events. They are evolving systems embedded in organizations and society. Managing them responsibly requires seeing the full chain, from data to consequences, and identifying every stakeholder along the way. As autonomy increases, transparency and accountability become more important, not less. Governance must expand as systems become more capable.

Emerging AI Laws, Regulations, and Standards

Governments, regulators, and standards organizations around the world are rapidly developing frameworks to govern artificial intelligence. These efforts reflect a growing recognition that AI systems can produce significant economic, social, and ethical consequences.

Most regulatory frameworks focus on AI *systems*—how they are designed, documented, deployed, and monitored. But accountability is exercised through AI *projects*. Project teams, therefore, play a central role in translating regulatory expectations into real practices.

An overview of major regulatory frameworks and standards is provided in Appendix B.

Why Projects Matter

These frameworks share a common insight: responsible AI requires governance throughout a system's lifecycle.

Yet governance does not occur in the abstract. It occurs through decisions made during projects: when data is selected, models are designed, interfaces are built, and deployment decisions are approved.

For this reason, the governance of AI systems ultimately depends on the governance of AI projects. Project teams must interpret regulatory expectations, identify affected stakeholders, and establish accountability before systems are deployed.

The following chapters introduce practical methods for identifying stakeholders, clarifying responsibilities, and managing the risks that arise when intelligent systems shape real-world decisions.

Chapter 2

When Machines Make Decisions

AI systems do more than provide information. In many cases, they shape or make decisions directly (OECD, 2019).

Some systems recommend. Others rank. Others classify. Some act automatically, without human approval.

The level of automation matters.

Human-in-the-Loop

In this model, a person reviews the system's output before making a final decision.

- A doctor reviews an AI-assisted diagnosis.
- A recruiter reviews a ranked list of candidates.
- A bank official reviews a credit score before approving a loan application.

Here, humans remain accountable, but they may rely heavily on the system (Green & Chen, 2019).

Even when final approval rests with a person, AI systems can subtly influence judgment, framing which options appear reasonable or efficient (Moser et al., 2022).

Human-on-the-Loop

In this case, the system acts automatically, but a human supervises it.

- Fraud detection systems that block transactions
- Content moderation tools that remove posts
- Logistics systems that reroute deliveries

Humans may intervene only when something goes wrong.

As automation increases, intervention becomes reactive rather than proactive. Oversight may exist in theory, but in practice humans often monitor exceptions rather than decisions themselves.

Human-out-of-the-Loop

Some systems operate fully autonomously.

- Automated trading systems
- Real-time threat detection
- Autonomous vehicles

In these systems, the algorithm makes decisions without waiting for human input.

Technically, such systems function as artificial agents. They act, respond, and adapt based on data and programmed objectives (Gibert & Martin, 2022). However, functional agency does not equate to moral agency. AI systems do not possess ethical intent or legal responsibility.

Accountability remains with the humans and organizations that design, deploy, and oversee them (Heaton et al., 2023).

As systems move further out of the human loop, responsibility does not disappear; it becomes distributed. Designers influence model behavior. Operators configure thresholds and deployment rules. Executives define objectives and acceptable risk levels. Each decision shapes outcomes, even if no single person makes the final call.

When autonomy increases, clarity of responsibility becomes more important, not less.

Why This Changes Stakeholder Risk

The more automated the system, the greater the distance between:

- The person who designed it
- The person who uses it
- The person affected by it

This distance creates what some call a "moral buffer" (Green & Chen, 2019).

Project teams may say:

> "We only built the tool."

Operators may say:

> "We only followed the system."

But the person harmed still experiences the consequence.

A moral issue exists whenever actions may harm or benefit others, even if decision-makers do not recognize the ethical stakes (Jones, 1991). AI systems themselves can influence, guide, or steer human judgment, even when humans believe they remain in control (Moser et al., 2022).

Responsibility in AI systems is therefore rarely concentrated in one role. It is distributed across designers, managers, deployers, and governing institutions (Heaton et al., 2023). When harm occurs, the question is not whether the machine is responsible, but how human responsibility was structured, assigned, and monitored.

Developers and deploying organizations are responsible for the foreseeable consequences of AI systems (Martin, 2019). AI projects must therefore clearly assign responsibility across all stages, especially as systems become more autonomous.

Part II

Why AI Projects Are Different

Chapter 3

The AI Lifecycle and When the Damage Appears

Traditional projects often measure success at delivery. If the system is built, delivered on schedule, and performs according to specification, the project is considered successful.

AI projects require a longer view (OECD, 2019).

Unlike traditional systems, AI systems continue to learn, adapt, and influence decisions after deployment. Their real-world effects often emerge only when the system begins interacting with people, institutions, and complex environments.

As a result, the most serious harms associated with AI projects frequently appear only after the project is considered complete.

The lifecycle of an AI system can be understood in three broad stages:

1. Development
2. Usage
3. Consequences

Each stage introduces different risks and affects different stakeholders.

Understanding when harm emerges is essential for responsible AI project management.

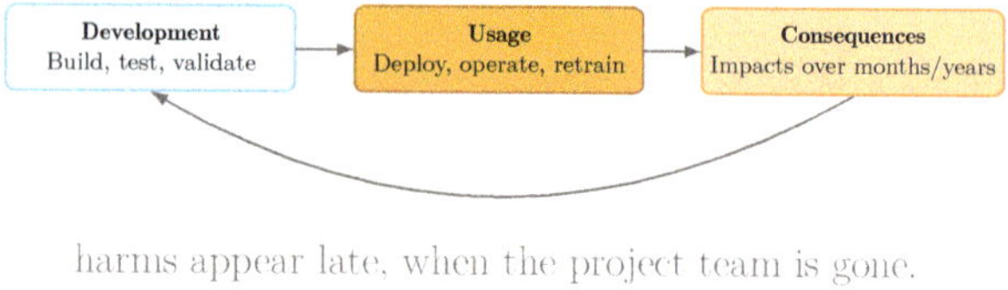

Figure 3.1: AI Project Lifecycle with distinct risk phases.

Stage 1: Development

The development stage includes the problem design, data selection, model construction, and evaluation of system performance.

During this stage, key risks include:

- Biased or incomplete training data
- Poor problem framing
- Lack of domain expertise

- Overconfidence in model accuracy
- Ignoring edge cases or unusual conditions

Many of the decisions that later shape harm are made here.

Choices about data sources, model objectives, evaluation metrics, and system boundaries determine what the system can see, what it can measure, and what outcomes it will prioritize.

Yet passive stakeholders are rarely present during development.

The individuals who may ultimately be affected by the system—customers, workers, citizens, or communities—are typically not consulted during this stage. Their interests may be represented only indirectly, if at all.

This creates an early asymmetry: decisions that affect future stakeholders are made before those stakeholders are even identified.

Stage 2: Usage

Once deployed, AI systems begin interacting with real users and real decisions.

During this stage, new risks emerge:

- Over-reliance on automated outputs
- Inadequate training for system users
- Lack of transparency about how decisions are made

- Poor escalation or override processes
- Gradual drift in model performance as environments change

Usage risks often reveal weaknesses that were not visible during development.

Even well-designed systems can cause harm if users misunderstand how the system works, treat probabilistic outputs as facts, or apply the system in contexts for which it was not designed.

Operational environments also introduce pressures that were not present during development. Users may prioritize speed, convenience, or efficiency over careful interpretation of system outputs.

For this reason, accountability does not end at deployment. Organizations must continue to monitor, evaluate, and justify system behavior after the system enters real-world use (Wieringa, 2020).

Stage 3: Consequences

The consequences of AI systems often appear gradually and may not be immediately visible.

Over time, patterns can emerge, such as:

- Systematic discrimination
- Loss of privacy or expanded surveillance
- Financial or reputational harm

- Job displacement or changes in working conditions
- Erosion of public trust in institutions
- Increased environmental or infrastructure strain

At this stage, the original project team may no longer be involved. The system may have been integrated into routine operations, scaled across organizations, or embedded in critical decision-making processes.

Yet the consequences remain linked to earlier project decisions.

Choices made during development and deployment determine how risks propagate through the system and who ultimately bears those risks.

For this reason, responsibility for foreseeable consequences remains with those who designed, approved, and deployed the system (Martin, 2019).

Why Timing Matters

The timing of harm has important implications for stakeholder management.

When harm emerges during the consequence stage, the individuals affected often direct their frustration toward the operators or frontline users of the system. These are the people they can see.

However, the root causes frequently trace back to earlier design choices:

- The data used to train the model
- The objectives encoded into the system
- The governance rules that allowed deployment
- The absence of safeguards for affected stakeholders

This means that stakeholder responsibility in AI projects cannot be limited to the point of use.

It must extend across the full lifecycle of the system.

> AI projects must anticipate future stakeholders, not only current ones.

Responsible teams, therefore, develop leading indicators of harm. They ask questions such as:

- Who could be affected by this system months or years after deployment?
- What assumptions might fail once the system encounters real-world conditions?
- How will we detect harm early?
- Who has the authority to pause, modify, or shut down the system if problems emerge?

These questions shift stakeholder management from reactive to proactive.

Instead of waiting for harm to appear, responsible teams design projects that actively monitor outcomes, incorporate feedback from affected stakeholders, and adapt governance as the system evolves.

Lifecycle awareness is therefore not only a technical concern. It is a governance discipline.

It ensures that responsibility for AI systems does not end when the project is delivered, but continues as long as the system continues to influence human decisions.

Chapter 4

Common Failure Patterns in AI Projects

Most AI failures do not result from malicious intent or deliberate misuse. They occur when risks affecting stakeholders are not fully understood during the design and deployment of a system.

AI systems are often developed by technically skilled teams working under time pressure, business incentives, and incomplete information. Decisions made during data collection, model development, and deployment can unintentionally create risks for people who were never part of the project.

Across industries, similar patterns recur.

These failures rarely result from a single mistake. Instead, they emerge when a series of small decisions accumulate across the lifecycle of a system.

Understanding these patterns helps project teams intervene before harm becomes visible.

Why Governance Fails in AI Projects

Many AI failures follow a similar governance pattern.

Projects typically begin with a focus on technical performance and business objectives. Passive stakeholders—those affected by the system but not involved in the project—often remain invisible during early design decisions. As a result, risks affecting these groups may not be considered when the system is created.

When stakeholder risks remain hidden, responsibility for potential harms also becomes unclear. Designers focus on model accuracy, project owners focus on deployment goals, and system users rely on automated outputs during operations. Each role contributes to the system, but no single role clearly owns responsibility for downstream consequences.

This creates a governance gap.

Across many AI projects, governance failures tend to arise from four connected weaknesses:

- **Stakeholder visibility gap**: Affected stakeholders are not identified early in the project
- **Responsibility gap**: Accountability for harms is unclear across project roles
- **Oversight gap**: Systems are deployed without adequate monitoring or review
- **Intervention gap**: Governance responses occur only after harm becomes apparent

Together, these gaps create a predictable cycle. Systems are designed and deployed before stakeholder risks are fully understood. Harm becomes visible only once the system begins influencing real-world decisions, at which point regulators, advocacy groups, or courts may intervene.

The failure patterns described in this chapter illustrate how these governance gaps appear in practice.

Failure Pattern 1: Biased or Incomplete Data

AI systems learn from data. If the data reflects past discrimination, structural inequality, or incomplete records, the system may reproduce those patterns (Chasalow & Levy, 2021).

Examples include:

- Hiring systems trained on historical employee data that reflects past hiring biases
- Credit models based on unequal lending history
- Predictive policing systems trained on past arrest records rather than underlying crime rates

Bias can also arise when datasets exclude important populations, rely on low-quality sources, or combine data collected for unrelated purposes.

In these situations, the system may appear statistically accurate while still producing unfair or harmful outcomes.

The risk is not only technical. It is also a stakeholder problem: the individuals most affected by biased outcomes are rarely present during the dataset development.

Failure Pattern 2: The Black Box Problem

Some AI models are difficult to interpret, particularly large machine learning systems that rely on complex statistical relationships rather than explicit rules.

When stakeholders cannot understand why a decision was made:

- Trust declines
- Appeals become difficult
- Errors are harder to diagnose
- Accountability becomes unclear

In highly automated environments, decisions may occur so quickly that neither users nor affected individuals can meaningfully question the outcome.

Algorithmic accountability therefore requires more than technical performance. It requires meaningful explanation and documentation of system behavior (Wieringa, 2020).

Transparency does not always mean revealing source code. It means providing understandable explanations of how the system works, what factors influence decisions, and how errors can be challenged.

Without this transparency, stakeholders may experience the system as an opaque authority rather than a tool subject to human judgment.

Failure Pattern 3: Automation Bias

Humans often trust automated outputs more than they should.

This phenomenon, known as "automation bias," occurs when people assume that algorithmic recommendations are more reliable than human judgment.

Even when a system is wrong, users may hesitate to override it.

This risk increases when:

- Performance metrics emphasize speed and efficiency
- Users lack training in system limitations
- The system presents outputs with high confidence
- Organizational culture discourages questioning automated tools

Automation bias can subtly shift decision authority away from humans and toward systems.

Users may become supervisors of automated processes rather than active decision-makers.

Algorithm-in-the-loop dynamics can therefore reduce critical oversight and allow errors to propagate through operational systems (Green & Chen, 2019).

Over time, responsibility may appear to shift from people to machines, even though the machine was designed, deployed, and governed by people.

Failure Pattern 4: Scope Creep of Impact

AI systems are rarely used only for their original purpose.

Once a dataset or model exists, organizations often discover new ways to apply it. Systems built for one context may gradually be reused in others.

For example:

- Data collected for marketing later used for risk scoring
- Security technologies repurposed to monitor employees or customers
- Analytical systems originally designed for operational efficiency later applied to financial or legal decisions

Each new use case may affect different stakeholders.

However, those stakeholders may never have been considered when the system was first designed.

This expansion of impact often occurs quietly, through incremental operational decisions rather than deliberate redesign.

Over time, the system may influence decisions far beyond the project's original scope.

Failure Pattern 5: Governance After Deployment

In many organizations, governance structures emerge only once problems arise.

Oversight committees, ethics reviews, and regulatory scrutiny are often triggered by incidents rather than built into the project from the beginning.

By the time governance mechanisms appear:

- Public trust may already be damaged
- Legal exposure may have increased
- Stakeholders may have experienced harm
- Correcting the system may become costly or politically difficult

Responsible governance requires anticipating these risks before deployment.

Organizations remain responsible for the foreseeable consequences of the systems they design and deploy (Martin, 2019).

This responsibility extends beyond technical performance to include how the system interacts with people, institutions, and social systems.

The lesson is simple:

> Engage stakeholders early, not only once harm occurs.

Projects that identify stakeholders only after deployment are reactive rather than proactive.

Effective AI governance, therefore, begins during project design, when decisions about data, objectives, and oversight structures are still flexible.

By recognizing common failure patterns early, project teams can build in stakeholder perspectives before systems reach the environments where harm becomes visible.

Part III

The Stakeholder Map

Chapter 5

The Six Roles That Shape AI Projects

Every AI project involves six stakeholder roles. Individuals or groups may hold more than one role, but the roles themselves are always present. Understanding these roles clarifies how responsibility is distributed across the life of an AI system.

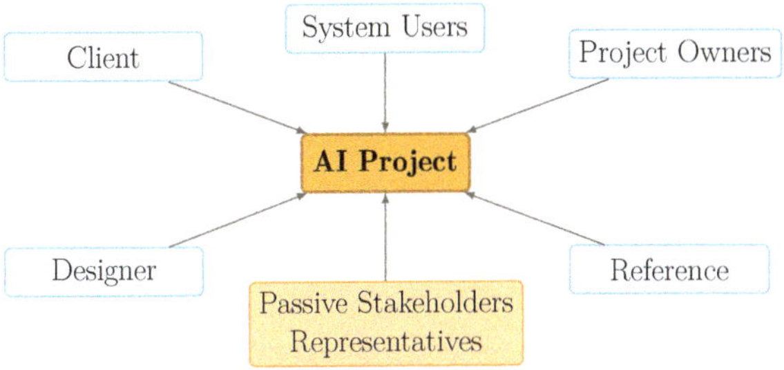

Figure 5.1: Six Stakeholder Roles present in every AI project.

Understanding these roles clarifies responsibility.

From Traditional Project Stakeholders to AI Project Roles

Project management research has long shown that stakeholders play a key role in project success (Davis, 2014; Turner & Zolin, 2012). Projects are more likely to succeed when stakeholder interests are identified and managed throughout the project lifecycle. However, research also shows that not all stakeholders participate equally. Some groups are directly involved in projects, while others have limited influence and remain largely passive.

The framework presented in this book builds on this research and adapts it to the specific context of artificial intelligence projects (Miller, 2022a). The six roles described in this chapter confirm many stakeholder groups identified in earlier studies while refining them for the realities of AI development.

The framework introduces several clarifications:

- **Distinguishing system users and passive stakeholders.** System users interact with AI outputs and apply them in operational decisions. Passive stakeholders may experience the consequences of those decisions even though they do not participate in the project.
- **Introducing the reference role.** Reference stakeholders, such as compliance officers, regulators, or ethics committees, do not design or operate the system; they provide guidance, interpretation, and oversight that shape project governance.

- **Expanding the concept of public stakeholders.** Building on earlier research, the framework explicitly recognizes groups affected by AI systems that often lack direct representation in projects. These passive stakeholders may include workers, decision subjects, vulnerable populations, local communities, or the environment.

These refinements address a broader question in AI governance: who is responsible for the outcomes of algorithmic decisions—the developer, the designer, or the system operator (Martin, 2019; Moser et al., 2022)?

The six-role framework provides a practical answer. By structuring projects around these roles, responsibility becomes clearer and easier to assign. Distinguishing between development actors, operational users, oversight roles, and passive stakeholders helps teams understand who shapes system behavior and who may be affected by its consequences.

The six roles described in this chapter, therefore, serve as a reference structure for stakeholder analysis throughout the remainder of this book.

1. The Client

The client is the organization that benefits from the AI system. It may be:

- A consumer
- A company deploying AI internally

- A government agency
- A platform operator
- A service provider

The client defines success and accepts the system for use.

2. System Users

System users are the people or organizations that rely on the AI system's outputs to make operational decisions.

They may include:

- Consumers
- End users
- Professionals such as doctors or recruiters
- Managers
- Organizational administrators

They decide how system outputs are used, even if they were not involved in building the system.

System users correspond to the human-in-the-loop and humar on-the-loop actors discussed in Chapter 2.

Whenever decisions may harm or benefit others, a moral issue exists, even if decision-makers do not explicitly recognize it (Jones, 1991).

System users convert algorithmic outputs into real-world actions. Even when the system provides recommendations, how those recommendations are interpreted and applied can directly affect individuals and communities.

3. Project Owners

Project owners have authority over the project and its deployment.

They control resources, define scope, and determine acceptable levels of risk.

They may include:

- Executive sponsors
- Program or project sponsors
- Steering committees
- Senior operational leaders

Project owners ultimately decide whether an AI system is built, deployed, or modified. They shape the system's purpose, scope, and governance. Their decisions determine where AI is deployed, what risks are considered acceptable, and what safeguards are required.

4. The Designer

Designers create the system. This group often includes:

- Data scientists
- Data engineers
- Software developers
- Architects

- Domain experts

Designers translate objectives into technical systems. Through choices about data, model design, and optimization criteria, they embed assumptions that shape how the system behaves in practice.

Designers shape systems that may later operate outside the human decision loop, as discussed in Chapter 2.

Developers and their organizations remain accountable for the downstream consequences of the systems they build (Martin, 2019).

5. The Reference Role

Reference stakeholders guide and support the project without owning it.

They may include:

- Legal advisors
- Ethics committees
- Compliance officers
- Data protection officers
- Internal governance teams

They provide oversight and interpretation.

6. Passive Stakeholders

Passive stakeholders may be affected by the system but have little or no influence over it.

Examples include:

- Data subjects
- Decision subjects
- Workers
- Vulnerable groups
- Local communities
- The environment.

They are central to ethical risk, even when absent from project meetings.

AI systems can reinforce structural inequities and disproportionately affect marginalized communities (Sambasivan et al., 2021).

Because passive stakeholders often lack power, they are frequently represented by other actors.

They may include:

- Regulators
- Courts
- Labor unions

- Advocacy groups
- Independent auditors
- Journalists

Representatives speak or act on behalf of passive stakeholders. Some have formal authority; others influence public opinion or policy.

Why These Roles Matter

Many AI failures occur because teams focus only on the roles closest to the project—clients, system users, project owners, and designers—while overlooking passive stakeholders and those who represent them.

Responsibility in AI systems is distributed across multiple actors. Designers shape system behavior. Project owners determine the system's purpose and governance. System users apply its outputs in real-world decisions.

Harm often occurs when these responsibilities are poorly defined or when each actor assumes that another is accountable.

Responsible AI use, therefore, requires identifying and including people who may be affected by the system, especially those who cannot represent themselves.

Chapter 6

Passive Stakeholders: The People You Don't Hear From

Passive stakeholders are often invisible during project planning. Yet they may experience the strongest impact.

They fall into three main categories.

1. Data Subjects

These are individuals whose data is collected, stored, or used to train models.

Risks include:

- Loss of privacy
- Data misuse
- Surveillance
- Profiling without consent
- Intellectual property infringement

Data subjects may not know their information is being used (Wieringa, 2020).

Bias and underrepresentation in datasets can distort outcomes and exclude entire communities from fair treatment (Chasalow & Levy, 2021).

2. Decision Subjects

These are individuals directly affected by system outputs.

For example:

- A person denied a loan
- A candidate rejected for a job
- A citizen flagged by law enforcement
- A patient misdiagnosed

Decision subjects may experience financial loss, reputational damage, restricted freedom, or even physical harm.

AI systems can reinforce existing structural inequities, particularly among marginalized populations (Sambasivan et al., 2021).

3. Workers

AI systems increasingly shape work dynamics.

Workers may experience:

- Psychological harm
- Algorithmic management

- Performance scoring
- Job displacement
- Psychological strain from content moderation

Some new jobs emerge, such as data labeling or moderation. But these roles may also involve stress or instability.

Societal Stakeholders

Beyond individuals, entire communities may be affected.

- Minority groups facing biased outcomes
- Local communities under surveillance
- The public affected by misinformation
- The environment impacted by energy-intensive model training

Large AI models require substantial computing power, which consumes energy and produces carbon emissions (OECD, 2019).

The community that benefits from AI may not be the one that bears its environmental cost.

The Core Challenge

Passive stakeholders often:

- Lack information
- Lack direct access to decision-makers

- Lack negotiation power
- Lack awareness of the system's existence

Without structured inclusion, their interests are easily overlooked.

Chapter 7

Representatives: Who Speaks for the Silent

Because passive stakeholders cannot always participate directly, representation becomes critical.

There are three main types of representatives.

Formal Representatives

These include:

- Regulators
- Courts
- Data protection authorities
- Labor unions

They have legal power. They can impose fines, restrict operations, or require corrective action.

For example, data protection laws may impose significant penalties for misuse of personal data (European Commission, 2016).

Advocacy Groups

These include:

- Non-governmental organizations
- Standards bodies
- Community boards
- Policy groups

They may not have formal authority, but they can influence policy, public perception, and reputation.

Algorithmic accountability increasingly requires organizations to explain, justify, and document how automated systems operate (Wieringa, 2020).

Independent Evaluators

Independent evaluators include:

- Auditors
- External reviewers
- Journalists
- Researchers
- Insurance providers

They may uncover bias, expose harm, or certify compliance.

Organizations remain responsible for the outcomes of their systems, even when third parties identify the risks (Martin, 2019).

When Representation Fails

Representation may fail when:

- Representatives are not invited early enough
- Their concerns are treated as compliance issues only
- Engagement occurs after deployment
- Feedback is ignored

Effective AI governance requires engaging representatives during development, not only after incidents occur.

Including Representatives in Practice

Project leaders can:

- Invite external experts during scope definition
- Include governance roles in steering committees
- Conduct impact assessments before deployment
- Establish review checkpoints tied to lifecycle stages

Representation should be proactive, not reactive.

Representation alone does not determine which stakeholders require attention. Project teams must first identify who may influence the project and who may be affected by the system. The next chapter introduces the *Four Tests*—power, legitimacy, urgency, and harm—which provide a structured method for identifying stakeholders and determining when representation may be necessary. Together, these tools help teams recognize not only who participates in a project, but also who may need protection when they cannot participate directly.

Chapter 8

The Four Tests: Power, Legitimacy, Urgency, and Harm

Identifying stakeholders in an AI project requires more than a brainstorming exercise.

Project teams usually recognize obvious stakeholders such as sponsors, engineers, and regulators. However, they often overlook individuals or groups who may experience the consequences of automated decisions.

To support systematic identification, this book introduces four tests that help determine whether a person or group should be considered a stakeholder and how much attention they may require.

The four tests are:

1. Power
2. Legitimacy
3. Urgency
4. Harm

Power Can they influence the project?	**Legitimacy** Is there a recognized obligation?
Urgency When are they impacted?	**Harm** Could they experience damage or loss?

Figure 8.1: The Four Tests for identifying and prioritizing stakeholders.

If a person or group meets at least one of these criteria, they should be considered a stakeholder.

Together, the four tests help project teams evaluate two critical dimensions of stakeholder analysis:

- **Influence**: stakeholders' ability to affect project outcomes

- **Exposure to harm**: the potential for stakeholders to be affected by system decisions

The framework builds on established stakeholder theory while extending it to address the specific governance challenges posed by artificial intelligence systems.

Extending the Stakeholder Salience Model

The Four Tests framework builds on the Stakeholder Salience Model developed by Mitchell et al. (1997), which classifies stakeholders according to three attributes:

- **Power**: the ability to influence project outcomes,
- **Legitimacy**: a socially accepted or rightful claim to attention,
- **Urgency**: the degree to which stakeholder claims require a immediate response.

Mitchell et al. (1997) proposed that all stakeholders possess at least one of these attributes and that the combination of attributes determines stakeholder salience. The model provides managers with a structured way to identify stakeholders and determine which groups deserve priority attention.

However, the original model has several limitations:

- It does not fully capture the dynamic nature of projects, where stakeholder influence and relationships can change over time (Eskerod & Huemann, 2013).
- It often prioritizes stakeholders who already hold organizational power, potentially overlooking groups whose interests may be affected but who lack influence (Derry, 2012).

This book extends the stakeholder salience model in three important ways to address these limitations and adapt it to AI projects.

- **Adding harm as a fourth attribute.** The framework introduces *harm* as an additional attribute for stakeholder inclusion. This inclusion recognizes that stakeholders may warrant attention not because they influence the project, but because they may experience negative consequences from the system.

- **Connecting urgency to the AI lifecycle.** The urgency attribute is interpreted across an AI system's lifecycle. Different stakeholders become relevant at different stages of development, usage, and long-term consequences. This places stakeholders on a time continuum that reflects when they are most likely to influence the project or assess its outcomes.

- **Recognizing long-term system impacts.** AI systems can produce consequences that appear months or years after deployment. Extending urgency across lifecycle stages supports the view that projects should anticipate delayed impacts and develop early indicators of potential harm.

Together, these adaptations transform the traditional salience model from a tool that primarily prioritizes influential stakeholders into a framework that also highlights those who may be affected by AI systems but lack direct power within the project.

The following sections describe each of the four tests—power, legitimacy, urgency, and harm—and explain how they can be applied to identify and prioritize stakeholders in AI projects.

Test 1: Power

Power refers to the ability to directly influence project decisions, resources, or outcomes.

Power does not always come from formal authority. It can take several forms:

- **Formal power**: authority derived from organizational roles.
- **Economic power**: control over funding, contracts, or procurement.
- **Expert power**: specialized technical or professional knowledge.
- **Coercive power**: the ability to impose penalties or sanctions.
- **Reputational power**: the ability to influence public opinion or institutional credibility.

Executives, regulators, and project sponsors typically have formal power. But journalists, auditors, advocacy groups, and influential customers may also shape project outcomes through reputational or economic influence.

Identifying power helps teams understand who can shape project decisions.

Test 2: Legitimacy

Legitimacy refers to a recognized relationship that gives a stakeholder a valid claim to consideration.

Legitimacy often arises through:

- Employment relationships
- Service agreements
- Customer relationships
- Regulatory mandates
- Legal rights
- Ethical obligations

For example, employees operating a system have legitimate interests in workplace safety and system reliability. Customers have legitimate expectations regarding fairness and service quality.

Legitimacy confers moral standing on stakeholders, even when they have little direct influence over project decisions (Jones, 1991).

Test 3: Urgency

Urgency reflects how quickly a stakeholder concern requires attention or response.

In AI systems, urgency is closely related to the stage of the system lifecycle where stakeholder interests become visible.

Three stages are particularly important:

- **Development**: designing and building the system.
- **Usage**: operating the system within organizational workflows.
- **Consequence**: the real-world effects produced by automated decisions.

Different stakeholders become relevant at different stages.

For example:

- Engineers and designers become urgent stakeholders during **development**.
- Operators and system users become urgent during **usage**.
- Decision subjects and affected communities may experience urgency only during the **consequence** stage.

However, urgency should not be interpreted only as the moment when harm becomes visible.

In many AI systems, the conditions that cause harm appear earlier in development or deployment. By the time consequences emerge, design decisions may already be difficult to change.

Responsible projects therefore treat urgency as a *forward-looking signal.*

Project teams should ask:

- Which stakeholders may experience consequences later?

- At what stage can their concerns still be addressed?

Recognizing delayed urgency allows teams to incorporate protections earlier in the lifecycle, when governance controls and design decisions remain flexible.

Test 4: Harm

The fourth test introduces an essential element of responsible AI governance.

Anyone who could experience harm from the system should be considered a stakeholder, even if they have no direct influence over the project.

Potential harms include:

- Physical harm or safety risks
- Loss of freedom or legal rights
- Loss of privacy or personal data exposure
- Financial damage
- Psychological stress
- Reputational damage
- Environmental impact

Traditional stakeholder models focus primarily on influence. However, AI systems often affect individuals who have little ability to shape project decisions.

Algorithmic accountability therefore requires attention not only to who has power, but also to who may be harmed (Wieringa, 2020).

Even without formal relationships or contracts, foreseeable harm creates a responsibility for organizations that design or deploy the system (Martin, 2019).

From Identification to Prioritization

The four tests help answer two critical questions:

- Who can influence the project?
- Who may be harmed by the system?

Some stakeholders influence project decisions directly through power or legitimacy. Others may have little influence but face significant exposure to harm from system outcomes.

Responsible AI governance requires attention to both.

Connecting the Four Tests to Stakeholder Prioritization

The four tests help project teams identify who should be considered a stakeholder. However, identification alone is not enough. Projects must also determine which stakeholders require the most attention during governance reviews.

In practice, the four tests reveal two important dimensions of stakeholder analysis.

- **Influence on the project.** Power, legitimacy, and urgency together indicate how strongly a stakeholder can influence project decisions, resources, or outcomes.

- **Exposure to harm.** The harm test identifies stakeholders who may experience the effects of a system even when they have little or no ability to influence how it is designed or used.

Figure 8.2 shows how the four tests connect these two perspectives. Power, legitimacy, and urgency combine to assess stakeholder influence, while the harm test identifies those exposed to the system's outcomes.

Putting the Four Tests Together

During a stakeholder workshop like the one described in Chapter 11, teams use the four tests to identify stakeholders and assess their relative importance.

Power, legitimacy, and urgency help estimate a stakeholder's influence on project decisions. Harm helps estimate how strongly the system's outcomes may affect them.

Together, these factors allow stakeholders to be positioned within the stakeholder analysis quadrant shown in Figure 8.3.

The quadrant helps teams distinguish four types of stakeholders:

- Those who influence decisions

- Those who must be kept informed

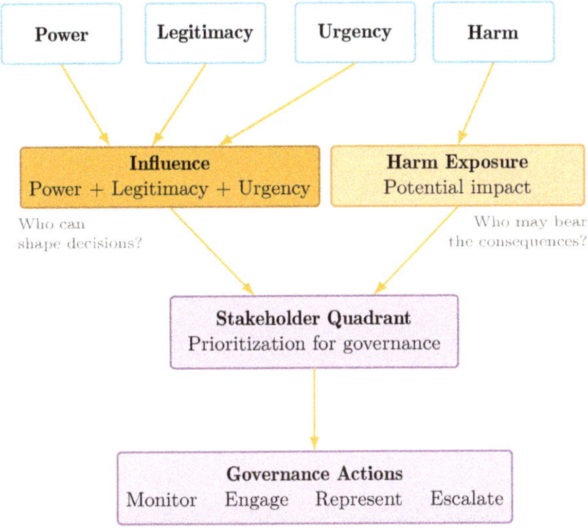

Figure 8.2: How the four tests connect stakeholder identification to governance actions.

- Those who require monitoring, and
- Those who may experience harm despite having limited influence

This final category is especially important.

In many AI systems, the individuals or communities most affected by automated decisions have the least ability to influence how those systems are designed or deployed.

When harm exists without representation, projects become vulnerable to ethical, legal, and reputational failure.

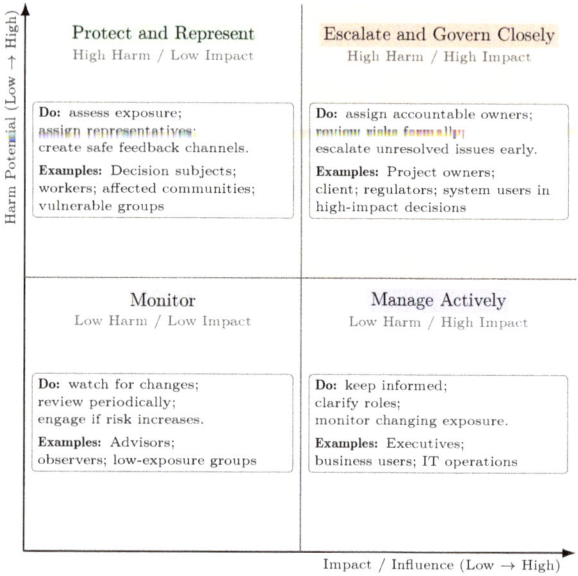

Note: stakeholders with low impact on project decisions may still require high governance priority if their potential exposure to harm is significant.

Figure 8.3: arm and Stakeholder Impact Quadrant for prioritizing stakeholders based on harm potential and impact on project decisions.

Stakeholder analysis is not only about who has influence. It is also about who may bear the consequences.

The stakeholder workshop described in Chapter 11 applies this process in practice. Teams identify stakeholders, apply the four tests, and then use the results to position stakeholders within the quadrant that guides governance action.

Part IV

When Things Go Wrong

Chapter 9

When Passive Stakeholders Are Harmed

This chapter presents a set of real-world cases in which AI or algorithmic systems caused harm to passive stakeholders. Table 9.1 provides an overview. The cases were selected to illustrate how harm can emerge at different points in the AI system chain—from data collection and model development through to deployment and real-world consequences.

For each case, the analysis considers three questions:

1. What was the background situation?
2. Which passive stakeholders were harmed?
3. Which project roles contributed to the harm, or could have helped prevent it?

The goal is not to assign blame, but to understand how stakeholder risks emerge and how they could have been addressed. These cases illustrate how stakeholder mapping can help identify where harm occurred, who was affected, and where responsibility should have been more clearly clearer.

Table 9.1: Overview of AI Lifecycle Stages, Passive Stakeholders, and Roles Implicated in the Case Studies.

Case	AI System Stage Implicated	Passive Stakeholders Harmed	Key Project Roles Involved
Pharmacy Facial Recognition	Source Data; Model Development; Decisions and Consequences	Decision Subjects; Data Subjects; Societal Stakeholders	Client; Project Owners; Designers; System Users
Copyright Data Use	Source Data; Training Data	Data Subjects	Designers; Project Owners; Reference Role
Interactive Brokers Trading	User Interface; Decisions and Consequences	Decision Subjects	System Users; Project Owners; Client
Auto Loan Trust	Data Collection and Storage; Decisions and Consequences	Workers; Small Business Operators	System Users; Project Owners; Client
GenAI Citation Misuse	User Interface; Decisions and Consequences	Decision Subjects; Societal Stakeholders	System Users; Designers; Reference Role

The cases presented in this chapter are derived from publicly available sources, including regulatory actions, court filings, and reported events. They are included solely to illustrate how stakeholder mapping can be applied when examining real-world AI projects.

These summaries are not intended to provide legal analysis or definitive conclusions about the events described. The cases have been simplified for educational purposes, and some details may be incomplete, contested, or subject to differing interpretations.

9.1 Pharmacy Facial Recognition Case

Background

Between 2012 and 2020, an American pharmacy retailer deployed an AI-based facial recognition system across hundreds of its stores in the United States. The system was intended to support store security by identifying individuals suspected of previously shoplifting or other problematic behavior (FTC, 2023).

To operate the system, the retailer created a database containing tens of thousands of images of individuals considered "persons of interest." These images were drawn from multiple sources, including security cameras, employee phone cameras, and publicly available materials such as news images. The system compared faces captured by store cameras against this database and generated alerts when a match was detected.

However, the system produced thousands of false-positive matches. Customers were repeatedly and wrongly identified as suspected shoplifters. Employees acted on these alerts by confronting individuals, ordering them to leave stores, searching them, and in some cases calling the police.

In December 2023, the U.S. Federal Trade Commission (FTC) determined that the pharmacy retailer had deployed the technology without adequate safeguards and banned the company from using facial recognition for surveillance for five years.

This case illustrates how governance failures can emerge across several stages of the AI system chain, including *data collection*, *model development*, and *real-world deployment*. Table 9.2 shows how the case maps to the system lifecycle, the passive stakeholders affected, and the project roles involved.

The events also reflects several governance gaps discussed earlier in this book: affected stakeholders were not identified during system design, responsibility for system outcomes was unclear across roles, and intervention occurred only after the system had already caused harm.

This case also illustrates the automation patterns introduced earlier. Designers created the matching algorithm (human-out-of-the-loop); supervisors oversaw its use in stores (human-on-the-loop); and employees acted on system-generat alerts (human-in-the-loop). Together, these layers created a "moral buffer." As a result, accountability was unclear to affected customers, who remained passive stakeholders.

Passive Stakeholders Harmed

The primary passive stakeholders harmed in this case were:

- **Decision subjects**: customers wrongly identified as shoplifters by the system
- **Data subjects**: individuals whose biometric images were collected and stored in the surveillance database

Table 9.2: Stakeholder Mapping and Governance Gaps in the Pharmacy Facial Recognition case.

Passive Stakeholder	**Harm Experienced**	**Role with Responsibility**	**Governance Gap**
Customers (Decision Subjects)	Wrongful accusations of theft due to incorrect facial matches	System Users; Client	Stakeholder Visibility Gap
Data Subjects	Collection and storage of biometric images without adequate safeguards	Project Owners; Designers	Oversight Gap
Communities	Discriminatory impacts and reputational harm	Client; Reference Role; Regulators	Intervention Gap

- **Societal stakeholders**: communities affected by discriminatory outcomes the technology produced

Customers had no control over the operation of the facial recognition system, yet its outputs directly determined how employees treated them. Many were unaware that biometric surveillance was taking place.

This reflects a *stakeholder visibility gap*. The individuals most affected by the system were not represented during the project that created and deployed the technology.

The FTC also found that the system disproportionately produced false positives in stores located in majority Black and Asian communities, raising broader concerns about fairness and discrimination.

How the Passive Stakeholders Were Harmed

The harms occurred through several mechanisms.

False accusations and humiliation

Customers wrongly flagged by the system were publicly accused of wrongdoing. Employees sometimes followed them through stores, searched them, ordered them to leave, or contacted law enforcement.

These confrontations occasionally took place in front of family members or other customers, causing reputational and emotional harm.

Privacy and biometric data risks

The retailer collected and stored tens of thousands of facial images without clearly informing customers or obtaining their consent. Many images were of poor quality and were drawn from various sources, increasing the likelihood of incorrect matches.

Discriminatory impact

The technology produced higher rates of false positives in stores located in communities with higher proportions of Black and Asian residents, creating unequal exposure to wrongful accusation on location and demographic profile.

These harms also point to an *oversight gap*. The system was deployed without sufficient testing, monitoring, or review mechanisms that could have detected these risks earlier.

Roles That Contributed to or Could Have Prevented the Harm

Client

The pharmacy retailer acted as the client: it defined the purpose of the system, approved its use for retail surveillance, and benefited from the deployment.

As the organization responsible for deployment, it was also responsible for establishing governance structures capable of evaluating the risks the system created.

Project Owners

Project owners approved deployment and were responsible for establishing governance controls. According to the FTC complaint, the retailer failed to adequately test, assess, and measure the accuracy of the technology before deploying it.

This reflects a *responsibility gap*: no single role clearly owned accountability for the downstream consequences of system errors.

Designers

The developers of the facial recognition system designed the algorithms used to match faces and generate alerts. Weaknesses in the technology—including poor performance with low-quality images—contributed to the high volume of false-positive matches.

Technical design decisions therefore contributed to the risk environment in which the system operated.

System Users

Store employees acted as system users, responding to alerts and interacting with customers based on system outputs. The FTC noted that employees were not adequately trained to understand the system's limitations and often treated alerts as reliable evidence of wrongdoing.

This reflects automation bias, which is the tendency of human decision-makers to place excessive trust in automated recommendations.

Reference Role

Regulators such as the FTC established the legal and ethical boundaries for deployment, but intervened only after significant harm had already occurred.

This illustrates an *intervention gap:* governance mechanisms were triggered only after the technology had already produced harmful outcomes.

Passive Stakeholder Representatives

Consumer protection groups, civil rights organizations, and regulators acted as representatives of passive stakeholders, raising concerns about misuse, discrimination, and lack of safeguards.

These actors effectively filled governance gaps that had not been addressed during the project itself.

9.2 Copyright Data Use Case

Background

Large language models require extremely large training datasets. In the early development of several AI systems, engineers assembled large text corpora by downloading books from online libraries such as LibGen and other publicly available repositories. These libraries contain millions of digitized books, many of which were uploaded without the authors' or publishers' permission.

In one widely discussed example, internal records showed that engineers downloaded hundreds of thousands of books from the Books3 dataset and millions more from other pirate libraries to build training datasets for AI models. These sources were attractive because they were easily accessible and avoided the cost and complexity of licensing large collections of books ("Bartz v. Anthropic PBC", 2025).

The books were stored in internal repositories and evaluated for use in training large language models. The authors later filed legal claims alleging that their copyrighted works had been copied and used without permission.

This case primarily involves the *source data*, *data collection and storage*, and *training data* stages of the AI system chain. Table 9.3 shows how the case maps to the system lifecycle, the passive stakeholders affected, and the project roles involved.

The case also illustrates several governance gaps discussed earlier in this book. Authors and other copyright holders were not identified as stakeholders during the early stages of dataset collection, responsibility for verifying the legal status of training data was unclear across project roles, and oversight mechanisms capable of reviewing training data sources were either weak or absent.

This case further reflects the automation patterns discussed earlier. Designers assembled the training datasets (human-out-of-the-loop); project owners and compliance functions should have supervised the sourcing process (human-on-the-loop); and direct human-in-the-loop involvement was limited, because the harm occurred before the system was deployed.

Table 9.3: Stakeholder Mapping and Governance Gaps in the Copyright Data Use Case.

Passive Stakeholder	**Harm Experienced**	**Role with Responsibility**	**Governance Gap**
Data Subjects (Authors)	Use of copyrighted texts for training without consent or compensation	Designers; Project Owners	Responsibility Gap
Authors and Content Creators	Loss of control over intellectual property and reproduction of creative work	Client; Designers	Stakeholder Visibility Gap
Public Knowledge Ecosystem	Potential erosion of creative incentives and economic sustainability for creators	Reference Role; Passive Stakeholder Representatives	Oversight / Intervention Gap

Passive Stakeholders Harmed

The primary passive stakeholders harmed in this case were:

- **Data subjects:** authors and copyright holders whose books were included in training datasets
- **Societal stakeholders:** the broader creative ecosystem, including publishers, researchers, and cultural institutions

These stakeholders were not involved in the development of the AI systems and were not consulted when their works were collected and incorporated into the training data.

This reflects a *stakeholder visibility gap.* The individuals whose creative works formed a large portion of the training data were not recognized as stakeholders in the project that collected and used the data.

How Passive Stakeholders Were Harmed

The harm occurred through several mechanisms.

Unauthorized reproduction of creative work

Books were copied and included in training datasets without the copyright holders' permission. Authors were not compensated for the use of their works.

Loss of licensing opportunities

If the AI developer had obtained licensed copies of the books, authors and publishers could have received payment for the use of their works. Instead, the datasets were obtained through pirate libraries.

Loss of control over creative content

Authors typically retain rights over how their works are reproduced and distributed. Incorporating books into AI training datasets removed that control and enabled their use in ways the creators did not authorize.

Systemic impact on the creative economy

When AI systems are trained on large collections of unpaid creative works, the resulting models may compete with the very creators whose work enabled their development.

These harms also reveal an *oversight gap*. The sourcing and ingestion of training data occurred without governance mechanisms capable of reviewing the legal and ethical implications of the datasets being used.

Roles That Contributed to or Could Have Prevented the Harm

Client

Organizations deploying AI systems often demand rapid innovation and competitive performance. These incentives can create pressure to obtain large training datasets quickly and at low cost. Without governance controls, such pressures may encourage the use of readily available datasets rather than properly licensed sources.

Project Owners

Project owners determine project scope and approve major decisions about data sourcing. By prioritizing speed and scale, they may implicitly allow the use of questionable data sources. In this case, responsibility for verifying the legal status of training data was not clearly assigned, reflecting a *responsibility gap*.

Designers

Engineers and data scientists selected and assembled the training datasets. In this case, designers downloaded large datasets from pirate libraries without verifying the material's legal status.

While the technical task of assembling datasets fell to the design team, governance responsibility for approving data sources should have extended beyond the technical role.

System Users

System users played a limited role in this case because the primary harm occurred before deployment, during dataset sourcing and ingestion, rather than during operational use of the AI system.

Reference Role

Legal advisors, ethics committees, and compliance officers could have identified intellectual property risks and required the use of licensed or public-domain datasets. However, these governance actors were either not involved early enough or lacked authority to influence dataset sourcing decisions.

This illustrates an *intervention gap.* Governance mechanisms capable of reviewing the decision emerged only after the issue became public through legal disputes.

Passive Stakeholder Representatives

Authors' associations, publishers, and copyright organizations later represented the interests of creators by filing legal claims and advocating for stronger protections.

These representatives effectively filled governance gaps that had not been addressed during the system's development.

9.3 Interactive Brokers Trading Case

Background

Automated decision systems are widely used in financial markets to manage trading accounts and respond to changing market conditions. One common application is the use of algorithms to automatically liquidate assets in margin accounts when account equity falls below required thresholds.

In this case, an investor alleged that an automated liquidation algorithm used by an online brokerage firm executed a series of trades that sold his securities at unfavorable prices after his account fell below margin requirements. The investor claimed that flaws in the algorithm caused his positions to be sold at prices significantly below market levels at the time, resulting in substantial financial losses ("Batchelar v. Interactive Brokers, LLC", 2019).

The case raised questions about whether the brokerage firm and the algorithm's developer had exercised reasonable care in its design and operation. The appellate court determined that the negligence claims warranted further consideration, finding that the lower court had not fully analyzed whether a duty of care existed in relation to the algorithm's design and operation.

This case primarily involves the *decision-and-consequences* stage of the AI system chain. Table 9.4 shows how the case maps to the system lifecycle, the passive stakeholders affected, and the project roles involved.

The case also illustrates governance gaps discussed earlier in this book. Investors affected by the automated system had little insight into how liquidation decisions were made, responsibility for the algorithm's performance was distributed across multiple organizational roles, and oversight mechanisms capable of detecting errors in real time were limited.

This case also reflects the automation patterns introduced earlier. Engineers designed the algorithm (human-out-of-the-loop), operational staff monitored the system (human-on-the-loop), and liquidation decisions were executed automatically without real-time human approval.

Passive Stakeholders Harmed

The primary passive stakeholders in this case were:

- **Decision subjects:** investors whose accounts were automatically liquidated by the algorithm

These investors did not design, control, or supervise the algorithm. Once their account values crossed the margin threshold, the system executed liquidation trades automatically and without prior notice.

Although investors were customers of the brokerage platform, they were effectively passive stakeholders in the algorithmic decision-making process. They had limited ability to understand or influence how the liquidation algorithm operated.

Table 9.4: Stakeholder Mapping and Governance Gaps in the Interactive Brokers Trading Case.

Passive Stakeholder	Harm Experienced	Role with Responsibility	Governance Gap
Retail Investors	Financial losses caused by automated liquidation trades executed at unfavorable prices	Client; Project Owners; Designers	Stakeholder Visibility Gap; Responsibility Gap
Market Participants	Distorted or unstable market activity caused by rapid automated liquidation actions	Project Owners; Designers	Oversight Gap
Financial System	Potential systemic risk when automated trading systems interact across markets	Reference Role; Regulators	Intervention Gap

This reflects a *stakeholder visibility gap.* While investors were directly affected by the system's decisions, their interests were not fully represented in the design and governance of the automated liquidation process.

How Passive Stakeholders Were Harmed

The harm occurred through the automated execution of trading decisions.

Automated liquidation of assets

When the margin threshold was triggered, the system executed liquidation trades automatically. The investor alleged that the algorithm sold positions at prices lower than those being obtained by other market participants at the same time.

Limited transparency in algorithmic decisions

The investor lacked insight into how the liquidation algorithm determined the trade timing or pricing. Without understanding the system's logic, it was difficult to challenge or prevent the outcomes.

Financial loss

Because the liquidation occurred automatically and rapidly, the investor suffered economic harm before any human review could occur.

These harms also reveal an *oversight gap*. Once the automated process was triggered, the system operated with limited real-time monitoring or mechanisms to pause or review the liquidation decisions before losses occurred.

Roles That Contributed to or Could Have Prevented the Harm

Client

The brokerage firm acted as the client and deploying organization. It benefited from the automated system and determined the operational model for margin account management.

As the deploying organization, it was responsible for establishing governance structures capable of evaluating the risks posed by automated trading systems.

Project Owners

Project owners determined the policies governing automated liquidation systems. They decided whether to deploy fully automated liquidation and which safeguards or oversight mechanisms to implement.

Where responsibility for monitoring algorithmic behavior is not clearly defined, this creates a *responsibility gap*.

Designers

Engineers designed the algorithm that determined how positions would be liquidated. If the algorithm contained programming flaws or failed to appropriately account for market conditions, those design choices directly contributed to harm.

However, technical design alone does not determine outcomes. Governance processes should ensure that automated decision systems are tested and reviewed before deployment.

System Users

Operational users within the brokerage firm monitored or supervised automated trading systems. In highly automated environments, however, they often intervene only after a problem has already occurred.

This dynamic illustrates the challenge of supervising automated systems that operate faster than human response times.

Reference Role

Compliance officers, risk managers, and legal advisors could mitigate harm by reviewing algorithmic trading systems and ensuring that safeguards are in place to protect investors.

In this case, oversight mechanisms were activated only after losses had already occurred, reflecting an *intervention gap* in the governance of automated financial systems.

Passive Stakeholder Representatives

Financial regulators and consumer protection authorities represent investors in markets where complex automated systems are used. They can establish standards for transparency, fairness, and reliability in automated trading systems.

Regulatory review therefore becomes an external governance mechanism when internal project governance fails to address stakeholder risks during system design.

9.4 Auto Loan Algorithm Case

Background

Financial technology companies increasingly use automated analytics systems to manage loan portfolios and assess financial risk. These systems often rely on proprietary algorithms that evaluate loan performance and determine borrowing capacity or payment allocations.

In this case, a financial technology company provided analytics and capital access services to automobile dealerships financing vehicle purchases through "Buy Here Pay Here" (BHPH) lending programs. Under a Master Receivables Agreement, dealerships could sell loan portfolios derived from customer auto financing contracts to a loan trust managed by the fintech firm ("Walter Auto Loan Tr. v. Track Motors, LLC", 2023).

According to the dealership, the fintech provider used a proprietary algorithm to calculate each dealership's borrowing base and determine how funds from loan portfolios were distributed. The dealership alleged that errors in this algorithm caused the system to miscalculate financial positions and wrongfully withhold funds owed to the dealership.

The dealership claimed that more than fifty of the sixty-two dealerships using the system were affected by similar issues, and that the algorithm continued to be used despite known errors.

This case primarily involves the *decision and consequences* stage of the AI system chain. Table 9.5 shows how the case maps to the system lifecycle, the passive stakeholders affected, and the project roles involved.

The case also illustrates several governance gaps discussed earlier in this book. Dealerships affected by the automated system had limited insight into how the algorithm calculated their borrowing base, responsibility for verifying the accuracy of those calculations was unclear across project roles, and oversight mechanisms capable of identifying algorithmic errors were insufficient.

This case further reflects the automation patterns discussed earlier: engineers designed the algorithm (human-out-of-the-loop), operational staff monitored financial outcomes (human-on-the-loop), and the fund distribution was determined automatically, without direct human approval.

Passive Stakeholders Harmed

The primary passive stakeholders affected in this case were:

- **Workers and small business operators:** dealership owners and operators who relied on the platform's automated calculations to manage their finances

Although the dealerships had entered into contractual relationships with the fintech provider, they had no ability to inspect, modify, or challenge the algorithm used to calculate their borrowing base.

Table 9.5: Stakeholder Mapping and Governance Gaps in the Auto Loan Trust case.

Passive Stakeholder	Harm Experienced	Role with Responsibility	Governance Gap
Workers / Small Dealership Operators	Financial losses caused by incorrect algorithmic calculations of borrowing bases and withheld funds	Client; Project Owners; Designers	Stakeholder Visibility Gap; Responsibility Gap
Borrowers	Reduced access to financing if dealership liquidity is constrained by automated portfolio calculations	Project Owners; Designers	Oversight Gap
Local Economies	Economic disruption when financing platforms affecting multiple dealerships malfunction	Reference Role; Regulators	Intervention Gap

Once the algorithm processed their loan portfolios, dealerships effectively became passive stakeholders in the automated decision-making process.

This reflects a *stakeholder visibility gap.* While the algorithm directly affected dealership finances, the interests of those stakeholders were not fully represented in the design and governance of the automated financial system.

How Passive Stakeholders Were Harmed

The harm resulted from automated financial calculations performed by the algorithm.

Wrongful withholding of funds

The dealership alleged that the algorithm miscalculated portfolio values and withheld funds owed to the dealership, including approximately $100,000 related to a single loan portfolio.

Opaque algorithmic decisions

Because the algorithm was proprietary, dealerships could not evaluate how the calculations were performed or why certain funds were withheld. Without transparency, affected stakeholders had limited ability to identify or challenge errors.

Systemic financial impact

The dealership alleged that algorithmic errors affected more than fifty dealerships across the platform, and that funds withheld by the algorithm were not clearly accounted for within the financial system.

These harms also reveal an *oversight gap*. The automated calculations continued to operate despite alleged errors affecting multiple participants, suggesting that monitoring or review mechanisms were insufficient to detect and correct problems early.

Roles That Contributed to or Could Have Prevented the Harm

Client

The fintech platform acted as the client organization deploying the system. Business incentives to automate financial analytics may favor rapid deployment and operational efficiency, but governance processes must ensure that automated systems affecting financial transactions are reliable, transparent and auditable.

Project Owners

Project owners determined the policies governing the algorithm and how it was applied to loan portfolios. Where responsibility for validating algorithmic performance is not clearly defined, this creates a *responsibility gap*.

Designers

Software engineers and data scientists designed the algorithm used to calculate borrowing bases. Flaws in design or implementation directly produced incorrect financial calculations.

However, technical design alone does not determine outcomes. Governance processes should require testing, auditing, and verification before such systems are deployed at scale.

System Users

Operational staff within the fintech platform relied on the algorithm to inform financial decisions affecting dealerships. In highly automated environments, users may treat system outputs as authoritative, allowing errors to propagate without independent verification.

Reference Role

Legal, compliance, and financial risk specialists could help mitigate harm by reviewing algorithmic systems and ensuring that calculations are transparent, auditable, and consistent with contractual obligations.

In this case, intervention appears to have occurred only after disputes arose, reflecting a *intervention gap* in the oversight of automated financial systems.

Passive Stakeholder Representatives

Industry regulators and financial oversight authorities represent the interests of market participants who rely on algorithmic financial systems. When internal governance fails to address stakeholder risks during system design, external oversight often becomes the mechanism through which accountability is enforced.

9.5 Generative AI Citation Misuse Case

Background

In 2023, attorneys in a personal injury lawsuit submitted a legal brief containing multiple fabricated case citations generated by a generative AI system ("Mata v. Avianca, Inc." 2023).

The attorneys had used a generative AI tool to assist with legal research. The system produced several citations that appeared plausible and were submitted as supporting precedent in a court filing. However, when the opposing legal team attempted to locate the cited cases, they discovered that many did not exist.

When questioned by the court, the attorneys initially relied on the AI system's own responses as confirmation that the cases were legitimate. The court determined that the citations were fabricated and sanctioned the attorneys for submitting misleading legal materials.

The case illustrates how generative AI systems can introduce false information into professional decision-making processes when outputs are not independently verified.

This case primarily involves the *user interface* and *decision-and-consequences* stages of the AI system chain. Table 9.6 shows how the case maps to the system lifecycle, the passive stakeholders affected, and the project roles involved.

The case also illustrates several governance gaps discussed earlier in this book. Stakeholders affected by the legal process had no insight into how generative AI outputs were used in preparing the brief, responsibility for verifying the accuracy of AI-generated citations was not clearly defined, and oversight mechanisms for AI use in professional workflows were absent or insufficient.

This case further reflects the automation patterns introduced earlier: developers created the generative AI system (human-out-of-the-loop), organizations adopted and governed its use (human-on-the-loop), and attorneys relied on its outputs within their professional workflow (human-in-the-loop).

Table 9.6: Stakeholder Mapping and Governance Gaps in the Generative AI Citation Misuse case.

Passive Stakeholder	Harm Experienced	Role with Responsibility	Governance Gap
Litigants	Legal arguments distorted by fabricated AI-generated case citations	System Users; Client	Stakeholder Visibility Gap; Responsibility Gap
Judicial System	Additional proceedings required to investigate false citations; strain on court resources	System Users; Project Owners	Oversight Gap
Public Trust in Legal Processes	Reduced confidence in the reliability of AI-assisted professional work	Designers; Project Owners; Reference Role	Intervention Gap

Passive Stakeholders Harmed

The primary passive stakeholders affected in this case were:

- **Decision subjects:** the litigants involved in the legal case
- **Societal stakeholders:** the judicial system and the public who rely on the integrity of legal proceedings

The plaintiff and the defendant relied on accurate legal arguments and verified precedents. Neither party had any control over how the attorneys conducted their legal research.

The broader judicial system also became a passive stakeholder, since courts rely on accurate legal citations to evaluate arguments and apply precedent correctly.

This reflects a *stakeholder visibility gap.* The individuals most affected by the outcome of the case had no representation in the design or governance of the AI-assisted research process.

How Passive Stakeholders Were Harmed

The harm occurred through the introduction of fabricated legal authorities into a formal judicial process.

Misleading legal arguments

The submission of nonexistent cases distorted the legal arguments presented to the court. If undetected, such errors could influence judicial reasoning and potentially affect case outcomes.

Procedural delays

The court was required to conduct additional proceedings to investigate the validity of the citations, increasing legal costs and delaying resolution of the case.

Erosion of trust in professional processes

The incident raised broader concerns about the reliability of AI-generated information in professional decision-making environments, particularly in law, where accuracy and verification are essential.

These harms also reveal an *oversight gap*. The use of generative AI in legal research proceeded without safeguards requiring independent verification of AI-generated citations before submission to the court.

Roles That Contributed to or Could Have Prevented the Harm

Client

The organization adopting the AI tool determined how it was integrated into professional workflows. Responsible adoption requires governance policies that define acceptable uses of generative AI and ensure that safeguards are in place for high-stakes tasks.

System Users

The attorneys acted as system users. They relied on the AI system to generate legal research and incorporated its outputs directly into a court filing. As the professionals responsible for the final submission, they had a duty to verify the accuracy of the information before presenting it to the court.

Project Owners

Organizations deploying AI tools in professional environments should establish clear policies governing their use. Where responsibilities for verification and accountability are not defined, a *responsibility gap* follows.

Designers

Developers of generative AI systems produce models that generate probabilistic outputs rather than verified facts. Designers could reduce risk by implementing stronger output warnings, citation verification features, or mechanisms that flag uncertain or unverifiable information.

Reference Role

Legal ethics bodies, courts, and professional regulatory organizations provide guidance on acceptable conduct when AI systems are used in professional work.

In this case, governance intervention occurred primarily after the problem surfaced in court proceedings, reflecting an *intervention gap.*

Passive Stakeholder Representatives

Judges and regulatory authorities act as representatives of societal stakeholders by enforcing standards that protect the integrity of legal processes.

When internal governance fails to manage the risks of AI use in professional environments, external oversight becomes the primary corrective mechanism.

Chapter 10
What the Cases Show Collectively

Taken together, these cases show that harm to passive stakeholders can emerge at any point in the AI system chain.

In some cases, harm began during source data collection, when authors and rights holders were not recognized as stakeholders. In others, harm emerged during system deployment or operational use, when customers, investors, business operators, or litigants were affected by automated decisions they could not inspect, challenge, or meaningfully influence. In professional settings, harm arose when human users relied on AI-generated outputs without adequate verification.

Although the cases span different industries and technologies, they reveal a consistent governance pattern.

Across the cases, four governance gaps appeared repeatedly.

- **Stakeholder visibility gap.** Affected stakeholders were not identified during early project design. As a result, their interests were not considered when data was collected, models were trained, or systems were deployed.

- **Responsibility gap.** Responsibility for potential harms was distributed across multiple project roles. Clients defined system objectives, designers built the technology, project owners approved deployment, and users operated the system. Because accountability was fragmented, no single role clearly owned responsibility for protecting affected stakeholders.

- **Oversight gap.** Systems were deployed without sufficient testing, monitoring, or review of stakeholder impacts. Governance processes focused primarily on technical performance rather than the broader consequences of system decisions.

- **Intervention gap.** In several cases, corrective action occurred only after harm became apparent. Regulators, courts, or advocacy groups intervened after stakeholders had already experienced financial loss, reputational damage, or procedural harm.

Together, these gaps explain why similar failures appear across very different AI applications. When stakeholders remain invisible, responsibility becomes diffuse, oversight weakens, and organizations respond only after harm has emerged.

The cases also demonstrate that stakeholder harm does not occur only at the point of use. It can originate in data sourcing, model design, interface design, operational use, or post-deployment monitoring. Stakeholder inclusion must therefore extend across the full lifecycle of an AI system.

Several practical lessons emerge from the cases.

- **Identify passive stakeholders early.** Stakeholder mapping should begin at project initiation, not after deployment. Teams should ask who may be affected by the system—even if those individuals are not customers, users, or sponsors.
- **Include stakeholders at the stage where risk begins.** When harm originates in data collection, affected data subjects and their representatives should be considered at that stage. When harm arises during deployment or operations, stakeholder inclusion must extend to affected customers, workers, or communities.
- **Use representatives when direct participation is not possible.** Passive stakeholders often cannot participate directly. In these situations, project teams should engage representatives such as regulators, civil rights organizations, consumer advocates, copyright bodies, professional associations, or ethics advisors.
- **Clarify responsibility for stakeholder protection.** Each role in the project lifecycle should have clearly defined responsibility for identifying, reviewing, and responding to stakeholder risks.

- **Prepare system users to question automated outputs.** Many harms were amplified because users treated system outputs as authoritative. Training and governance procedures should emphasize verification, escalation, and the continued exercise of human judgment.
- **Monitor stakeholder impacts after deployment.** Stakeholder inclusion is not a one-time activity. Organizations should monitor for indicators that stakeholders may be experiencing harm, including both system-generated signals such as false positives and stakeholder-initiated ones such as complaints and appeals.

The central lesson is straightforward:

> When passive stakeholders remain invisible in AI projects, governance gaps emerge—and those stakeholders are the ones most likely to bear the consequences of system failure.

Effective AI governance therefore requires identifying who may be affected, ensuring their interests are represented, and assigning clear responsibility for protecting them through out the system's lifecycle.

Part V

Stakeholder Mapping Method and Tools

Chapter 11

The Stakeholder and Responsibility Mapping Workshop

This chapter presents a structured process for identifying stakeholder risks and clarifying responsibilities before deploying an AI system.

The *AI Stakeholder and Responsibility Mapping Workshop* helps teams:

- Identify who may be affected by an AI system
- Clarify responsibility across the AI lifecycle
- Detect hidden governance gaps
- Anticipate harm before it becomes systemic

The workshop follows a structured eight-step process and can typically be completed in 60–90 minutes.

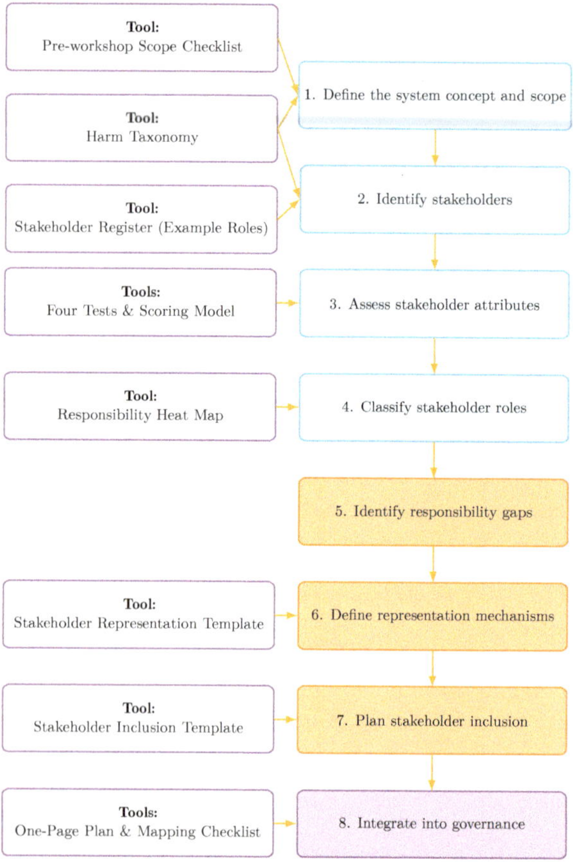

Figure 11.1: AI Stakeholder and Responsibility Mapping Workshop Flow with Supporting Tools.

Printable templates for the Stakeholder Register, Representation Plan, Inclusion Plan, and One-Page AI Stakeholder Plan worksheet are provided in Chapter 12.

Figure 11.1 summarizes the workshop flow and highlights the tools available to support each step. These tools are introduced throughout this chapter in text boxes labeled *Tool.*

The workshop focuses on the early stages of the AI system lifecycle, where stakeholder risks can still be identified and addressed before deployment.

11.1 Step 1: Define the Project Clearly

Begin by clearly defining the scope and purpose of the system under discussion.

Participants should agree on the system boundary and the decisions that the AI system will influence.

Write down:

- The purpose of the AI system
- The decisions it supports or automates
- The expected benefits
- The acceptable level of risk

Clarity at this stage prevents ambiguity later in the workshop.

Tool

Pre-work Scope Definition Checklist (Table 12.1: Used at the beginning of the stakeholder workshop to confirm that the AI system, its purpose, scope, and decision context are clearly defined before stakeholder analysis begins.

11.2 Step 2: Identify Stakeholders Across the AI Lifecycle

AI systems affect stakeholders across the three lifecycle stages described in Chapter 3: development, usage, and consequences.

- **Development stakeholders** — those who design and build the system (sponsors, project managers, engineers, legal and compliance teams).

- **Usage stakeholders** — those who operate or interact with the system during use (users, operators, maintainers).

- **Consequence stakeholders** — individuals or groups affected by system outcomes (decision subjects, communities, regulators, and the public).

Projects should adapt the stakeholder list to their specific context.

Tool

The Harm Taxonomy (Table 12.2): Provides a structured list of potential harms that may arise from artificial intelligence systems, including restrictions on freedom, denial of services, financial loss, privacy violations, psychological stress, discrimination, reputational damage, or environmental impact.

During early project definition, the taxonomy can serve as a screening tool to cross-check whether a proposed AI system could create foreseeable harms.

During the stakeholder workshop, it helps teams consider how system decisions could negatively affect individuals, communities, or the environment and ensures that potential harms are not overlooked.

The taxonomy can also support governance reviews by helping teams identify impact indicators that should be monitored after deployment.

Step 2a: Individual Brainstorming

Each participant should first brainstorm stakeholders individually before sharing with the group.

Ask:

> Who could be affected by this system—directly or indirectly—at any stage of its lifecycle?

Encourage participants to consider downstream and indirect impacts, not only those visible during development.

Step 2b: Consolidate the Stakeholder List

Combine the individual lists into a shared stakeholder register.

Duplicate entries should be merged, and unclear stakeholders clarified.

> **Tool**
>
> **The Stakeholder Register (Example Roles)** (Table 12.3): Provides a reference list of common stakeholders in AI projects.
>
> Use it to stimulate brainstorming during stakeholder identification and to cross-check whether important stakeholder groups have been overlooked.

11.3 Step 3: Assess Stakeholder Attributes

Apply the Four Tests described in Chapter 8 to each stakeholder group.

Ask:

- Do they have power to influence the project?
- Do they have legitimacy—a valid claim to consideration?
- When does urgency apply?
- Could they experience harm if the system fails or behaves incorrectly?

Stakeholders are evaluated visibly so that differences in perception can be discussed.

This step often reveals an important pattern:

> Some stakeholders face significant potential harm but have limited ability to influence project decisions.

These stakeholders require particular attention in governance planning.

Tool

Stakeholder Scoring Model (Chapter 12.4): Extends the Stakeholder Register by providing a structured method for estimating stakeholder influence and exposure to harm using power, legitimacy, urgency, exposure, severity, and scale. *Its use is optional.*

The resulting scores help position stakeholders within the harm–impact quadrant used to prioritize governance attention. The model can be applied during stakeholder workshops to support structured discussion and produce a stakeholder map such as the quadrant shown in Figure 8.3.

Tool

Lifecycle-Weighted Stakeholder Scoring (Chapter 12.5): An alternative scoring approach that refines the urgency attribute by evaluating stakeholder concerns across development, usage, and consequence stages of the AI lifecycle. *Its use is optional.*

This method provides a more detailed governance analysis when stakeholder risks emerge at different stages of the system lifecycle.

11.4 Step 4: Classify Stakeholder Roles

Stakeholders should be classified according to how they interact with the system based on the six roles described in Chapter 5.

- **Project Owners**: responsible for governance and approval decisions.
- **Designers**: engineers, data scientists, and architects who design the system.
- **Client**: the organization deploying or sponsoring the system.
- **System Users**: individuals who operate or rely on system outputs.
- **Reference Roles**: regulators, auditors, legal advisors, and oversight bodies.
- **Passive Stakeholders**: individuals or groups affected by outcomes but with limited influence over the project.

For workshop analysis, teams may optionally group these roles into:

- Active roles (owners, designers, reference roles)
- Operational roles (client and system users)
- Passive stakeholders

Passive stakeholders often include decision subjects, workers affected by automated decisions, and communities exposed to broader system impacts.

The relationship between stakeholder roles, lifecycle stages, and risk exposure is summarized in Figure 11.2. It illustrates how responsibility and risk shift across the AI lifecycle, often placing the greatest exposure on stakeholders who have the least influence over project decisions.

Tool

AI Stakeholder Responsibility Heat Map (Figure 11.2): Visualizes how responsibility, influence, and risk exposure shift across stakeholder roles and stages of the AI lifecycle.

The heat map highlights that different stakeholders shape the system during development, operate it during use, and experience its consequences after deployment. It helps project teams recognize where responsibility is concentrated, where risk exposure is greatest, and where passive stakeholders may face harm despite having limited influence over project decisions.

Stakeholder Role	Development	Usage	Consequences	Typical Risk Exposure
Project Owners	High influence	Medium	Medium	Strategic, governance
Designers	High responsibility	Low	Low	Technical performance, bias
Client	Medium	High influence	Medium	Operational, reputational
System Users	Low	High exposure	Medium	Operational decision errors
Reference Roles	Oversight	Oversight	Oversight	Compliance, regulatory
Passive Stakeholders	Low visibility	Medium exposure	High exposure	Social, economic, reputational

Risk gradient: Low Medium High

Figure 11.2: Lifecycle Stage, Stakeholder Roles, and Typical Risk Exposure Heatmap.

11.5 Step 5: Identify Responsibility Gaps

For stakeholder groups with high potential harm, ask:

- Who is responsible for preventing harm?
- Who monitors outcomes after deployment?
- Who has the authority to intervene if harm occurs?

If no clear owner exists, governance is incomplete.

The purpose of this step is to ensure that accountability is clearly assigned and can be traced across decisions made throughout the AI lifecycle.

11.6 Step 6: Define Representation Mechanisms

Passive stakeholders often lack direct influence in project decisions.

For stakeholders identified in Step 3 as having high potential harm but low influence, identify how their interests will be represented. Chapter 7 describes the types of representative roles that should be considered.

Possible mechanisms include:

- External advisors
- Regulators or oversight bodies
- Civil society organizations
- User advocacy groups
- Independent auditors
- Ethics review boards
- Impact assessments

Representation ensures that vulnerable stakeholders are considered even when they cannot participate directly.

Tool

Stakeholder Representation Template (Table 12.7): Documents how stakeholder groups—particularly passive stakeholders who may face harm but have limited influence—are represented during project decision-making.

The plan identifies the type of engagement, the project phase in which representation occurs, the individuals or organizations acting as representatives, and the evidence demonstrating that stakeholder concerns were considered.

This tool helps ensure that vulnerable stakeholders are not overlooked and that representation mechanisms are embedded within project governance.

11.7 Step 7: Plan Stakeholder Inclusion

For each stakeholder group, define:

- The inclusion method
- The project phase in which engagement will occur
- The responsible owner
- The resources required, including time, budget, and personnel.

Inclusion activities should be explicitly budgeted and scheduled rather than assumed.

Structured documentation and review are central elements of algorithmic accountability (Wieringa, 2020).

> **Tool**
>
> **Stakeholder Inclusion Template** (Table 12.8): Documents how stakeholder groups are actively engaged during an AI project.
>
> The plan specifies the inclusion method, the representatives or proxies involved, the lifecycle stage at which engagement occurs, and the evidence demonstrating that stakeholder input was considered. It also records the expected cost of inclusion activities to ensure that engagement is planned and resourced rather than treated as an informal or optional task.

11.8 Step 8: Lifecycle Integration

The workshop should produce a one-page stakeholder register documenting system purpose, stakeholder roles, risk exposure, and governance checkpoints. It includes:

- Stakeholder group
- Lifecycle stage
- Stakeholder role
- Risk level
- Responsible owner

- Budget for engagement
- Escalation authority

The register should be reviewed at each governance checkpoint or stage-gate review.

Stakeholder identification is not a one-time exercise; it must evolve as the system evolves.

Tool

One-Page AI Stakeholder Plan (Figure 11.3): A printable worksheet that helps project teams capture the essential elements of stakeholder governance in a single view.

It summarizes the system purpose, key decisions, stakeholder groups, potential harms, governance checkpoints, and monitoring metrics. The worksheet documents the outcomes of the Stakeholder and Responsibility Mapping Workshop and serves as a reference during project reviews and stage-gate decisions.

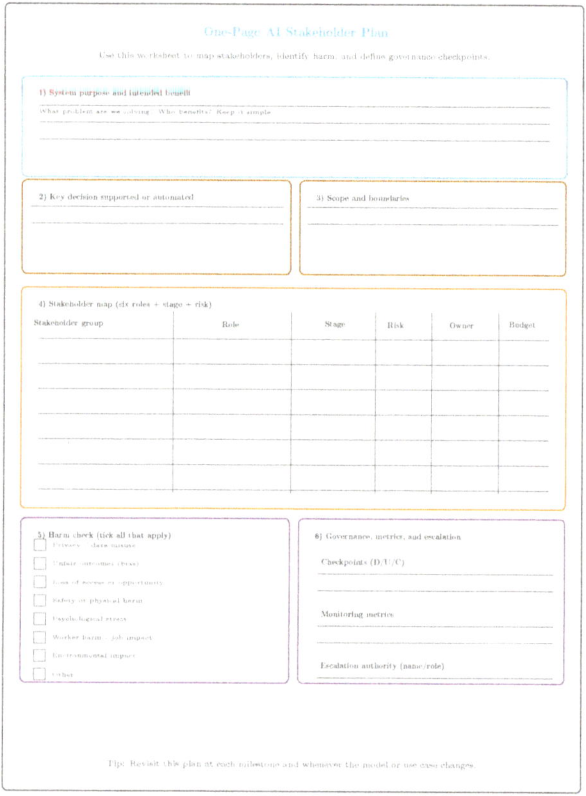

One-Page AI Stakeholder Plan

Use this worksheet to map stakeholders, identify harm, and define governance checkpoints.

1) System purpose and intended benefit

What problem are we solving? Who benefits? Keep it simple.

2) Key decision supported or automated

3) Scope and boundaries

4) Stakeholder map (six roles + stage + risk)

Stakeholder group	Role	Stage	Risk	Owner	Budget

5) Harm check (tick all that apply)

- ☐ Privacy / data misuse
- ☐ Unfair outcomes (bias)
- ☐ Loss of access or opportunity
- ☐ Safety or physical harm
- ☐ Psychological stress
- ☐ Worker harm / job impact
- ☐ Environmental impact
- ☐ Other

6) Governance, metrics, and escalation

Checkpoints (D/U/C)

Monitoring metrics

Escalation authority (name/role)

Tip: Revisit this plan at each milestone and whenever the model or use case changes.

Figure 11.3: **Printable worksheet.** Photocopy or print for workshops.

11.9 Common Mistakes to Avoid

- Treating stakeholder analysis as a compliance exercise
- Identifying stakeholders only during development
- Involving representatives too late
- Assigning responsibility without authority
- Focusing only on technical performance

Tool

AI Stakeholder Mapping Checklist (Table 12.9): A practical validation tool for the Stakeholder and Responsibility Mapping Workshop.

The checklist summarizes the key steps in identifying stakeholders, assessing risk exposure, assigning responsibility, and integrating stakeholder oversight into project governance. Teams can use it to verify that important stakeholder groups—particularly passive stakeholders who may face harm but have limited influence—have been properly considered before deployment.

11.10 A Final Reminder

The goal is not perfection.

The goal is transparency, clarity of responsibility, and proactive governance.

When harm is possible, silence becomes a governance risk.

Chapter 12

Stakeholder Analysis Tools

The stakeholder workshop described in Chapter 11 provides a structured method for identifying stakeholders, assessing potential harms, and clarifying responsibilities across the lifecycle of an AI system.

This chapter presents practical tools that support that process. Some tools help teams prepare for the workshop by confirming that the system scope and context are clearly defined. Others support stakeholder identification, harm analysis, and responsibility mapping during the workshop itself.

The tools are intentionally simple. Their purpose is to guide structured discussion and documentation, not to replace professional judgment. Used together, they help teams apply stakeholder analysis as a consistent governance practice.

How to Use the Tools The tools in this chapter appear in several formats, each supporting a different part of the workshop process.

- **Templates** provide structured outlines for documenting results such as stakeholder registers, representation plans, and inclusion plans.
- **Checklists** help teams confirm that key preparation and mapping steps have been completed.
- **Reference tables** illustrate common examples, such as stakeholder roles or types of potential harms.
- **Analytical tools** describe simple scoring approaches used to evaluate stakeholder influence and potential harm across the system lifecycle.

These tools are intended to support stakeholder workshops and governance reviews. Teams may adapt them to align with their organization's existing project management, risk management, or compliance practices.

12.1 Pre-workshop Scope Checklist

Table 12.1: AI System Scope Checklist used before the stakeholder workshop to confirm the project scope and system purpose are clearly defined.

Checklist Item	Key Questions	Done
Define System Purpose	What organizational objectives or benefits are expected? What outcomes should the system improve or enable? What problem is the system intended to solve?	☐
Define Intended Users	Who is expected to interact with or operate the system? How will system outputs be used in operational decisions?	☐
Identify Data Sources	What types of data will the system use? Where will the data originate (internal systems, external sources, or third parties)?	☐
Define Decision Context	Will the system recommend decisions, support human judgment, or automate outcomes? What level of human oversight is expected?	☐
Potential Harm Screening	Could incorrect or biased system outputs cause financial loss, denial of services, privacy violations, or other harm? Could system decisions affect vulnerable individuals or communities?	☐
Risk Classification Screening	Could the system affect safety, legal rights, employment, finance, healthcare, or public services? Does the system appear to fall into a regulated or high-risk AI category?	☐
Identify Regulatory Context	Are there known regulatory or compliance requirements affecting the system? Does the system operate in a regulated domain such as finance, healthcare, employment, or public services?	☐
Document Assumptions	What assumptions have been made about data quality, system performance, or operational context? Are there constraints or limitations that should be documented before analysis begins?	☐

12.2 Harms Taxonomy

AI systems can create harms across multiple stakeholder levels, including individuals, organizations, communities, and society at large. The taxonomy groups potential harms according to the stakeholder levels most directly affected. The was developed through a review of academic and policy literature on artificial intelligence harms[2]

Table 12.2: Taxonomy of AI Harms across stakeholder levels

Category	Examples of Potential Harm
AI System Workers	
Labor Exploitation	Low-paid global digital labor performing data labeling and moderation tasks for AI systems
Psychological Harm	Exposure to disturbing content such as violence, pornography, or hate speech while performing AI training data labeling or content moderation
Individuals	
Biometric Surveillance Without Consent	Collection and storage of facial images or biometric data without consent or adequate notice
Employment Loss	Automation replacing jobs or biased hiring algorithms excluding qualified candidates
Financial Loss	Algorithmic credit scoring errors, AI-enabled fraud, automated insurance pricing discrimination
Loss of Freedom / Wrongful Imprisonment	Incorrect facial recognition matches leading to wrongful arrest, detention, or imprisonment
Loss of Recourse or Appeal	Individuals affected by automated decisions cannot challenge or appeal outcomes due to opaque algorithms or lack of human review

Continued on next page

Table 12.2 – continued from previous page

Category	Examples of Potential Harm
Physical Harm	Autonomous vehicle failures, unsafe medical AI decisions, malfunctioning robotics causing injury or death
Privacy Loss	Facial recognition surveillance, mass biometric tracking, unauthorized data collection
Psychological Harm	Emotional distress caused by opaque automated decisions or AI-enabled harassment
Reputational Harm	False accusations generated by AI systems (e.g., facial recognition misidentification) leading to public humiliation or damage to personal reputation
Wrongful Law Enforcement Interaction	Incorrect algorithmic identification leading to police stops, searches, or detention of innocent individuals
Organizations	
Algorithmic Opacity	Organizations affected by automated decisions cannot inspect or understand how proprietary algorithms produce outcomes
Financial Loss	Cyberattacks enabled by AI systems or faulty automated decisions causing financial damage
Legal Liability	Discrimination lawsuits or regulatory penalties due to biased algorithms
Operational Harm	AI system failures disrupting critical services such as finance, healthcare, or logistics
Professional Liability Risk	Professionals relying on AI outputs (lawyers, doctors, analysts) may unknowingly submit incorrect information generated by AI systems
Reputational Damage	Public backlash from unethical AI use or biased decision systems
Strategic Damage	Over-reliance on automation or flawed models producing poor strategic decisions
Local Communities	

Continued on next page

Table 12.2 – continued from previous page

Category	Examples of Potential Harm
Creative Market Displacement	AI systems trained on copyrighted works may compete with creators whose content was used in training datasets
Economic Harm	Regional unemployment due to automation of local industries
Environmental Damage	Energy-intensive AI infrastructure affecting local environmental resources
Information Harm	AI-generated misinformation affecting public discourse and local elections
Institutional Trust Loss	Reduced trust in local government services relying on opaque automated decisions
Loss of Intellectual Property Control	Creators lose control over how their works are reproduced or incorporated into AI training datasets
Social Harm	Algorithmic policing disproportionately targeting specific communities
Society at Large	
Democratic Harm	AI-generated propaganda and misinformation influencing elections and public opinion
Economic Inequality	Automation increasing wealth concentration and labor displacement
Environmental Impact	Energy consumption of large-scale AI models and data centers
Institutional Trust Erosion	Incorrect or fabricated AI-generated information undermines trust in professional systems such as courts, journalism, or education
Procedural System Disruption	False AI outputs introduce delays and additional costs in legal or regulatory processes
Security Risk	Autonomous weapons or AI-enabled cyber warfare
Systemic Economic Risk	Algorithmic trading failures or automated market manipulation

12.3 Stakeholder Register (Example Roles)

A sample stakeholder register with example roles and including attributes for influence and harms for scoring.

Table 12.3: Extended Stakeholder Register with example roles and influence and harm scoring

		Influence			Harms			Scoring	
Stakeholder / Group	Notes on Impact or Exposure	P	L	U	E	S	Sc	Impact	Harm
Project Sponsor / Executive	Approves funding, strategic direction, and deployment decisions.								
Project Manager / Program Lead	Coordinates delivery, governance checkpoints, and risk management.								
AI Engineers / Data Scientists	Design models, select training data, and influence system behavior.								
Legal / Compliance Team	Interpret regulatory obligations and review governance controls.								
System Operators / Analysts	Operate the system in production environments and interpret outputs.								
Business Users / Customer Service Staff	Depend on system outputs to support operational decisions.								
System Maintainers / IT Operations	Responsible for reliability, updates, monitoring, and system retraining.								

Continued on next page

Table 12.3 – continued from previous page

Stakeholder / Group	Notes on Impact or Exposure	Influence			Harms			Scoring	
		P	L	U	E	S	Sc	Impact	Harm
Decision Subjects (Individuals evaluated by system)	Receive automated decisions or recommendations generated by the system.								
Customers / Clients	Experience system outcomes through products, services, or interactions.								
Regulators / Supervisory Authorities	Oversee compliance with legal obligations and investigate incidents.								
Civil Society / Advocacy Groups	Represent the interests of vulnerable populations or affected groups.								
Affected Communities / Public	May experience indirect impacts such as fairness concerns or social effects.								

Scoring scale: 0 = none, 5 = very high
Influence: P = Power, L = Legitimacy, U = Urgency
Harms: E = Exposure, S = Severity, Sc = Scale
Impact score = (P + L + U) / 3   Harm score = (E + S + Sc) / 3

12.4 Stakeholder Impact-Harm Scoring Model

When many stakeholders are involved, project teams often struggle to determine which stakeholders require the most governance attention.

To support consistent analysis, this chapter introduces a simple scoring model that helps teams estimate two factors:

- stakeholder **impact or influence on project decisions**
- stakeholder **potential exposure to harm**

These scores can be used to position stakeholders within the harm–impact quadrant introduced in Chapter 8 and shown in Figure 8.3.

The scores provide a structured approximation intended to support discussion during stakeholder workshops or governance reviews.

Power, Legitimacy, and Urgency

The power, legitimacy, and urgency attributes can be scored on a scale from 0 to 5.

Estimating Stakeholder Impact

Stakeholder impact can be estimated using the following formula:

Score	Interpretation
0	None
1	Very Low
2	Low
3	Moderate
4	High
5	Very High

Table 12.4: Stakeholder Attribute Scoring Scale

$$Impact = \frac{Power + Legitimacy + Urgency}{3}$$

The result produces a score between 0 and 5 representing the stakeholder's influence on project decisions.

Estimating Harm Potential

To estimate harm potential, teams may evaluate three factors:

- **Exposure**: the degree to which the stakeholder interacts with the system
- **Severity**: the seriousness of possible harm
- **Scale**: the number of individuals potentially affected

The harm score is calculated as:

$$Harm = \frac{Exposure + Severity + Scale}{3}$$

The result produces a score between 0 and 5 representing the degree stakeholders may be harmed by project outcomes.

Mapping Stakeholders in the Quadrant

These two scores provide the dimensions used in the stakeholder prioritization quadrant.

Once both scores are calculated, stakeholders can be positioned within the harm–impact quadrant.

Harm	Impact	Governance Response
Low	Low	Monitor
Low	High	Manage Actively
High	Low	Protect and Represent
High	High	Escalate and Govern Closely

Table 12.5: Governance Response to Harm and Impact Scoring

Worked Example

The following example shows how the Impact–Harm scoring model can be used during a stakeholder workshop.

Consider an AI system used to screen job applicants.

One stakeholder group is **job applicants**. Applicants do not participate in the project and have no influence over how the system is designed. However, the system may affect whether they are screened out or allowed to continue in the hiring process.

Step 1: Score Power, Legitimacy, and Urgency The project team assigns scores based on the stakeholder's influence and involvement during the development stage of the project.

- Power = 0 (job applicants have no direct influence over the project)
- Legitimacy = 5 (they have a clear right to fair evaluation)
- Urgency = 2 (applicants are not involved in development, but the project team recognizes their interests)

The impact score is calculated as:

$$Impact = \frac{Power + Legitimacy + Urgency}{3}$$

$$Impact = \frac{0 + 5 + 2}{3} = \frac{7}{3} = 2.33$$

The stakeholder impact score is approximately **2.3**.

Step 2: Estimate Harm Potential The team evaluates the potential harm the stakeholder could experience if the system performs poorly.

- Exposure = 4 (job applicants interact directly with the system)
- Severity = 4 (incorrect screening may hinder employment opportunities)
- Scale = 5 (many applicants may be affected)

The harm score is calculated as:

$$Harm = \frac{Exposure + Severity + Scale}{3}$$

$$Harm = \frac{4+4+5}{3} = \frac{13}{3} = 4.33$$

The stakeholder harm score is approximately **4.3**.

Step 3: Position the Stakeholder The stakeholder scores are:

- Impact = 2.3
- Harm = 4.3

This places job applicants in the **high harm/low impact** area of the quadrant.

According to Table 12.5, this suggests the governance response:

Protect and Represent

Although job applicants have no influence over the project, the potential harm they may experience is significant. The project team may therefore consider including a representative voice during system design or governance review.

For example, the team could consult an external advisory group, a labor representative, or an ethics committee to help ensure that applicant interests are considered when the system is designed and evaluated.

This example illustrates how the scoring model can identify stakeholders who require protection even when they have little direct influence over the project.

12.5 Stakeholder Lifecycle–Weighted Scoring Model

In AI projects, risks do not emerge evenly across the system lifecycle or across stakeholder groups. Some risks appear during development, while others emerge only after deployment when system decisions begin affecting individuals, organizations, or communities.

The urgency attribute can therefore be refined to reflect *where* stakeholder concerns arise within the AI lifecycle. This chapter introduces a lifecycle-weighted stakeholder scoring approach that refines the urgency attribute used in the Stakeholder Impact-Harm Model described in Chapter 12.4.

Rather than treating urgency as a single value, this approach evaluates urgency across multiple lifecycle stages and weights them according to their governance significance.

Lifecycle Urgency

Three lifecycle stages are particularly relevant for governance analysis:

- **Development** — system design, model creation, and data preparation
- **Usage** — operational use of the system within organizational processes
- **Consequences** — real-world impacts experienced by affected stakeholders

These stages do not carry equal governance weight.

Errors during development can often be corrected before deployment. Problems during system usage may disrupt operations but can sometimes be mitigated through monitoring or operational controls. Harms that emerge during the consequence stage, however, may directly affect individuals or communities and can be significantly more difficult to reverse.

Consequence-stage urgency therefore receives the greatest weight in governance analysis.

Lifecycle Urgency Formula

Lifecycle urgency can be estimated using the following weighted formula:

$$U = 0.2D + 0.3U_s + 0.5C$$

Where:

- D = development-stage urgency
- U_s = usage-stage urgency
- C = consequence-stage urgency

This weighting reflects the increasing governance importance of risks that materialize later in the system lifecycle.

Governance Impact Formula

Lifecycle urgency can then be incorporated into the stakeholder influence score.

$$Impact = 0.45P + 0.35L + 0.20U$$

Where:

- P = Power
- L = Legitimacy
- U = Lifecycle urgency

Power receives the greatest weight because it most directly affects project decisions and governance authority. Legitimacy reflects the strength of the stakeholder's claim to consideration, while lifecycle urgency captures the timing and potential escalation of stakeholder concerns.

Combined Governance Formula

Substituting the lifecycle urgency formula produces the full governance scoring model:

$$Impact = 0.45P + 0.35L + 0.20(0.2D + 0.3U_s + 0.5C)$$

This formulation ensures that stakeholders who may be affected during the consequence stage receive greater attention during governance analysis.

Governance Interpretation

The resulting impact score provides a structured estimate of how strongly a stakeholder should be considered in governance decisions.

Impact Score	Governance Response
0–2	Monitor
2–3.5	Engage and Review
3.5–4.5	Manage Closely
4.5–5	Escalate Through Governance

Table 12.6: Governance Interpretation of Lifecycle Impact Scores

This model provides a structured method for prioritizing stakeholder attention during governance reviews. Scores should support discussion and analysis rather than replace professional judgment.

Worked Example

The following example shows how lifecycle-weighted scoring can help project teams understand when stakeholder concerns become most important.

Consider an AI system used to screen job applicants.

One stakeholder group is **job applicants**. Applicants do not participate in the project and have no influence over how the system is designed. However, the system may strongly affect their employment opportunities.

Step 1: Score power and legitimacy. The team first estimates the stakeholder's power and legitimacy.

- Power $P = 0$ (job applicants have no direct influence over the project)
- Legitimacy $L = 5$ (they have a clear right to fair evaluation)

Step 2: Understand concern across the lifecycle. Stakeholder concern often shifts across the system lifecycle.

Job applicants are typically unaware that the AI system is being developed, so their concern during the development stage is effectively zero.

During system usage, applicants may care about the application process, such as whether the system is easy to use. However, these concerns are usually secondary.

The greatest concern arises during the consequence stage, when the system may screen out an applicant or allow them to proceed. This decision directly affects employment opportunities.

Step 3: Score lifecycle urgency. Based on this reasoning, the team assigns urgency scores for each lifecycle stage.

- Development-stage urgency $D = 0$ (applicants are typically unaware of the system)
- Usage-stage urgency $U_s = 2$ (application experience matters but is not critical)

- Consequence-stage urgency $C = 5$ (screening decisions strongly affect employment opportunities)

Step 4: Calculate lifecycle urgency. The lifecycle urgency formula is:

$$U = 0.2D + 0.3U_s + 0.5C$$

Substituting the values:

$$U = 0.2(0) + 0.3(2) + 0.5(5)$$

$$U = 0 + 0.6 + 2.5 = 3.1$$

The lifecycle urgency score is approximately **3.1**.

Step 5: Calculate the governance impact score. The governance impact formula is:

$$Impact = 0.45P + 0.35L + 0.20U$$

Substituting the values:

$$Impact = 0.45(0) + 0.35(5) + 0.20(3.1)$$

$$Impact = 0 + 1.75 + 0.62 = 2.37$$

The final impact score is approximately **2.4**.

Step 6: Interpret the result. According to Table 12.6, a score between 2 and 3.5 suggests the following governance response:

> **Engage and Review**

Although job applicants have no direct influence over the project, their concerns become very important during the consequence stage, when system decisions affect employment outcomes.

The project team may therefore consider including a representative voice during system design or governance review—for example, an external advisory group, a labor representative, or an ethics committee—to help ensure that applicant interests are considered before the system is deployed.

This example illustrates how lifecycle-weighted scoring identifies stakeholders whose concerns arise later in the system lifecycle, even when they have little awareness or influence during earlier stages.

12.6 Stakeholder Representation Template

The template below can be used to document how stakeholder interests are represented across the AI project lifecycle.

Table 12.7: Stakeholder Representation Template

Stakeholder	Engagement Type	Phase	Representative	Evidence
	Direct / Proxy	Concept / Design / Deployment		Meeting records, consultation notes, review memos

12.7 Stakeholder Inclusion Template

The template below can be used to document how stakeholder groups will be engaged throughout the AI project lifecycle.

Table 12.8: Stakeholder Inclusion Template

Stakeholder	Inclusion Method	Repre-sentative / Proxy	Lifecycle Stage	Evidence	Estimated Inclusion Cost
	Workshop Consult Audit Survey				

12.8 Stakeholder Mapping Checklist

The checklist summarizes the key steps of the AI Stakeholder and Responsibility Mapping Workshop. Teams can use it to confirm that stakeholder risks and governance responsibilities have been properly addressed.

Table 12.9: AI Stakeholder Mapping Checklist for responsible AI project governance.

Checklist Item	Key Questions	Done
Define the AI System	What decision does the system support or automate? What benefits are expected? What level of risk is acceptable?	☐
Identify Lifecycle Stakeholders	Who is involved during development? Who operates the system during usage? Who may be affected by system consequences?	☐
Apply the Four Tests	Do stakeholders have power? Do they have legitimacy? When does urgency apply? Could they experience harm?	☐
Identify High-Risk Stakeholders	Which stakeholders have **high potential harm** but **low influence**? Are these groups visible to project leadership?	☐
Map Stakeholder Roles	Who acts as project owner, designer, client, system user, reference role, and passive stakeholder?	☐
Identify Responsibility Gaps	Who prevents harm? Who monitors system outcomes? Who has authority to intervene?	☐
Define Representation Mechanisms	How are passive stakeholders represented? Do external advisors, regulators, or advocacy groups need to be involved?	☐
Plan Stakeholder Inclusion	How will stakeholders be engaged? Who is responsible for inclusion activities? Are time and budget allocated?	☐
Integrate into Governance	Is a stakeholder register maintained? Will stakeholder mapping be reviewed at stage-gate checkpoints?	☐

Part VI

Governance and Oversight

Chapter 13

Governance That Works in the Real World

13.1 Why Governance Matters

The cases in the previous chapter show that many AI failures are not caused by bad intentions or misuse. They happen when teams fail to clearly define responsibility, oversight, and stakeholder risks during project design and deployment.

The cases span retail surveillance, AI training data, financial trading systems, lending analytics, and generative AI in legal work. Despite their differences, the same governance problems appeared. In each situation, stakeholders were affected by system decisions even though they had no involvement in the project that created the system.

These cases reveal a recurring set of governance gaps.

- Stakeholders affected by the system were not fully identified.

- Responsibility for risks was distributed across multiple roles.
- Oversight mechanisms appeared only after deployment.
- Harm became apparent only when the system affected real-world decisions.

In each situation, governance failed not because rules were missing, but because responsibility and stakeholder risks were not adequately clarified during key project decisions.

The stakeholder workshop described in Chapter 11 addresses the first gap. It helps teams identify affected stakeholders, possible harms, and responsibility during project design.

Governance addresses the remaining challenges.

This distinction matters in AI projects because automated systems may influence decisions long after a project ends.

> Governance ensures that decisions remain traceable, risks are addressed early, and accountability remains clear.

Governance defines how authority, accountability, and oversight function within a project. It determines:

- Who makes decisions
- What information supports those decisions
- How risks are escalated

- How system outcomes are monitored over time

This structure is especially important because AI systems may influence decisions long after delivery. When responsibility is unclear, problems may emerge months or years later. This often affects stakeholders who were never consulted during the project.

Governance does not replace stakeholder management. Stakeholder management focuses on relationships and inclusion; governance provides the structure that ensures these responsibilities are carried out.

As AI systems gain autonomy, research consistently shows that accountability remains with the humans and organizations that design, deploy, and oversee them (Heaton et al., 2023).

Figure 13.1 shows how the governance gaps identified in the case studies connect to the stakeholder and governance approaches presented in this book.

The governance framework presented in this chapter is organized around six practical principles. Each principle addresses specific governance gaps and is supported by practical tools that help organizations document decisions, monitor impacts, and respond to emerging risks.

Figure 13.2 summarizes these principles and the tools that support them.

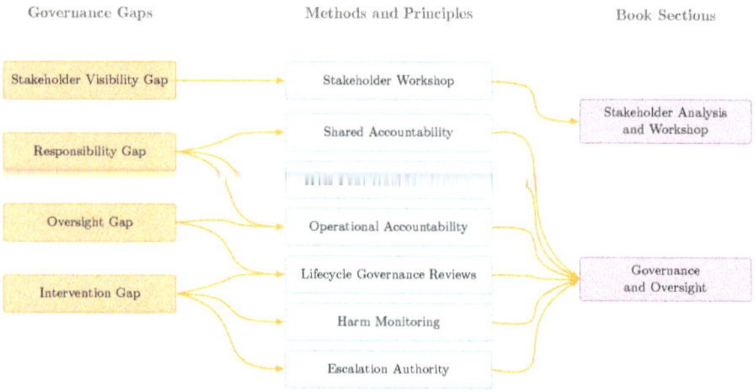

Figure 13.1: Governance Gaps in AI projects, the methods and principles that address them, and where they are developed in this book.

13.2 Principle 1: Shared Accountability

Define who is responsible for:

- Data quality
- Model performance
- Ethical review
- Regulatory compliance
- Post-deployment monitoring

Responsibility should not end when the project closes (Martin, 2019).

Responsibility for AI systems rarely belongs to just one role. Governance must clearly define who is responsible for each key decision and outcome.

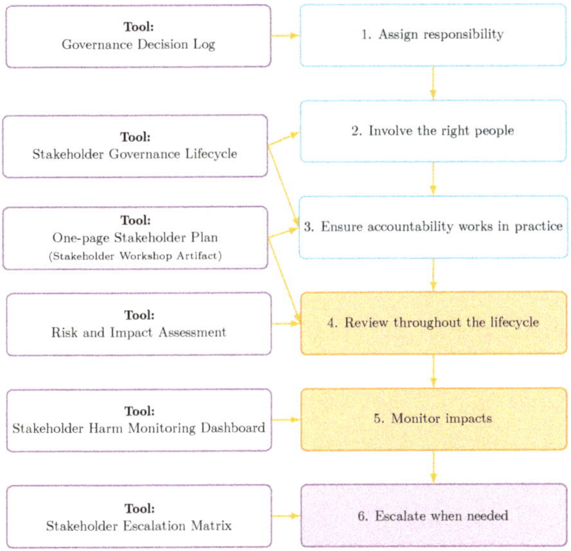

Figure 13.2: Governance Principles and Tools that support their application across the AI lifecycle.

Without clear assignment, accountability becomes fragmented

Tool

Governance Decision Log (Table 14.5): Records major governance decisions, the stakeholders considered, the risks reviewed, and the authority responsible.

It helps maintain clear accountability and supports traceability across the AI system lifecycle.

13.3 Principle 2: Cross-Functional Involvement

AI projects should include:

- Technical experts
- Business leaders
- Legal advisors
- Risk and compliance officers
- External advisors when needed

Different perspectives reduce blind spots, but they do not always appear naturally.

Technical and management perspectives tend to dominate AI projects. End users and affected communities are less often included in governance decisions (Kuehnert et al., 2025). Broader participation can strengthen legitimacy and trust, but is often constrained by time, budget, and institutional barriers.

Recognizing these structural limits is the first step toward designing governance processes that are both realistic and inclusive.

> **Tool**
>
> **Stakeholder Governance Lifecycle** (Table 14.1): Maps where stakeholder identification, representation, and monitoring activities occur across the AI system lifecycle.
>
> Project teams can use it to ensure that stakeholder risks identified during the workshop are carried forward beyond system development and are reviewed during deployment, operational use, and beyond.

13.4 Principle 3: Operational Accountability

Assigning formal roles does not guarantee that responsibility will be exercised in practice.

Research on AI projects shows that accountability is often diffuse across project owners, managers, and technical teams. Responsibilities that look clear in governance documents can become fragmented in everyday decisions.

In complex AI systems, multiple actors influence outcomes simultaneously:

- Engineers shape model behavior
- Product teams define operational objectives
- Managers approve deployment decisions
- Operators configure real-world usage

When governance focuses only on formal role definitions, responsibility can become diluted across these actors.

Effective governance therefore requires tools that turn formal responsibility into everyday practice:

- Decision logs
- Documented model approvals
- Incident review processes
- Traceable change management

These mechanisms ensure that responsibility remains traceable even when decision authority is distributed across teams.

13.5 Principle 4: Lifecycle Governance Reviews

Introduce review checkpoints tied to lifecycle stages:

- Pre-development impact assessment
- Pre-deployment review
- Early-usage performance review

- Periodic consequence evaluation

Each stage should include stakeholder reassessment.

Tool

The Risk and Impact Assessment (Table 14.2) documents potential risks, stakeholder exposure, and governance responsibilities before an AI system is deployed.

It draws on governance practices recommended by the NIST AI Risk Management Framework, ISO/IEC 42001, and the EU AI Act. It helps organizations evaluate potential harms, confirm stakeholder protections, and document accountability before deployment.

This tool is not intended to function as a regulatory compliance checklist. Organizations should apply their own internal governance procedures and consult relevant regulatory requirements when performing formal risk assessments or conformity evaluations.

Clear documentation and regular reviews are central to algorithmic accountability (Wieringa, 2020).

Stage-gate reviews also create formal opportunities to revisit assumptions, especially when stakeholder voices were limited during initial design.

Reviews should consider system capabilities, not only lifecycle timing.

Different AI capabilities introduce different governance risks:

- Generative systems raise concerns about fabricated information
- Predictive systems raise concerns about bias and fairness
- Automated decision systems raise concerns about transparency and appeal rights

Governance reviews should therefore examine how system functionality shapes stakeholder risk and adjust oversight accordingly.

13.6 Principle 5: Harm Monitoring

Measure more than accuracy.

Track indicators such as:

- Complaint rates
- Appeal outcomes
- Error disparities across groups
- Environmental metrics
- Worker impact metrics

Monitoring must extend beyond technical performance to include social and organizational signals that may show early signs of harm.

> **Tool**
>
> **Stakeholder Harm Monitoring Dashboard** (Table 14.3) helps teams track indicators that may signal emerging stakeholder harm after deployment.
>
> It supports the governance principle that monitoring should extend beyond technical performance to include social, organizational, and stakeholder impacts.

13.7 Principle 6: Escalation Authority

Ensure someone has authority to:

- Pause deployment
- Adjust models
- Investigate incidents
- Notify affected stakeholders

Without escalation authority, governance becomes symbolic.

Escalation processes should also define who can act when harm affects stakeholders who have limited influence; governance should reduce power imbalances, not reinforce them.

Escalation paths should also recognize that some risks extend beyond the organization.

Tool

Stakeholder Escalation Matrix (Table 14.4) defines when stakeholder-related risks should be escalated, who has the authority to act, and what response is required.

It helps project teams connect incident severity and stakeholder harm to appropriate governance action.

13.8 Governance as a Response to Failure Patterns

The governance principles described in this chapter respond directly to the failure patterns observed in the case studies.

In many AI projects, responsibility becomes fragmented across technical teams, managers, and operational users. Stakeholder concerns may arise during early discussions but gradually disappear from decision-making as projects move toward deployment.

The governance framework addresses these risks by establishing mechanisms that sustain responsibility, oversight, and stakeholder protection throughout the system lifecycle.

Together, these principles turn stakeholder analysis into a practical governance system that guides project decisions.

13.9 Governance Across the AI Lifecycle

AI risks do not emerge at a single moment. They can arise during system design, during operational use, or long after deployment, when automated decisions begin to affect individuals and communities.

Governance must therefore extend across the full lifecycle of an AI system.

Lifecycle reviews, harm monitoring, and escalation processes ensure that stakeholder risks identified during design continue to be monitored after deployment, when real-world impacts begin to appear.

13.10 Governance Under Delivery Pressure

Governance structures are most vulnerable when organizations face strong delivery pressures.

Research on AI projects shows that accountability for ethics, compliance, and societal impact often weakens when teams prioritize rapid delivery or cost reduction.[3]

In these situations, governance processes may still exist on paper but carry less influence on actual decisions.

Effective governance therefore requires mechanisms that remain robust under pressure:

- Independent risk review
- Protected escalation channels
- Documented decision accountability

- Incentives that do not reward speed over safety

These safeguards help ensure that accountability does not erode when project timelines accelerate.

> Effective governance is not about eliminating risk entirely. It is about making responsibility visible, distributing authority clearly, and ensuring that stakeholder concerns can be heard before harm becomes systemic.

Chapter 14

Governance Tools

Chapter 13 explained how governance structures help ensure that responsibility, oversight, and accountability remain visible throughout the lifecycle of an AI system.

This chapter introduces practical tools that support those governance practices. Some tools help teams document decisions and confirm that responsibilities are clearly assigned. Others support lifecycle reviews, risk monitoring, and escalation when issues arise.

The tools are intentionally simple. Their purpose is to support consistent governance discussions and documentation rather than replace professional judgment. When used together, they help project teams apply governance principles in a structured and repeatable way across AI projects.

How to Use the Tools The governance tools in this chapter appear in several formats, each supporting a different governance activity.

- **Templates** provide structured formats for documenting governance decisions, responsibilities, and oversight mechanisms.
- **Checklists** help teams confirm that governance activities have been completed at key stages of the project lifecycle.
- **Reference tables** summarize governance practices that help clarify roles, accountability, and escalation paths.
- **Analytical tools** support structured evaluation of risks, stakeholder impacts, and system oversight needs.

These tools are designed to support governance reviews throughout the lifecycle of an AI system. Teams may adapt them to align with existing project governance, risk management, or compliance practices within their organization.

14.1 Stakeholder Governance Lifecycle

Table 14.1 is a **Stakeholder Governance Lifecycle** that visualizes where stakeholder identification, representation, and monitoring activities occur across the AI lifecycle.

The map connects stakeholder analysis to the three lifecycle stages—development, usage, and consequences—and highlights when governance actions such as stakeholder identification, representation planning, and harm monitoring should occur.

Teams can use the map during project initiation to confirm that stakeholder risks, representation mechanisms, and oversight responsibilities have been considered from a lifecycle perspective, not only during system development.

Table 14.1: AI Governance across the system lifecycle

Stage & Activity	Stakeholder Roles Involved	Governance Focus
Development Stage		
Project Initiation and Scope Definition	Client, project owners, designers, passive stakeholder representatives	Identify stakeholders and potential harms; clarify project objectives, decision authority, and representation gaps
Pre-Development Impact Assessment	Project owners, designers, reference roles, affected stakeholders	Evaluate potential impacts, stakeholder risks, and escalation triggers before development begins
Training Data Review	Designers, domain experts, reference roles, affected stakeholder representatives	Assess dataset provenance, representation gaps, privacy risks, and potential bias
Model Testing and Validation	Designers, system users, reference roles, specialized stakeholder groups	Evaluate fairness, safety, usability, and the adequacy of human oversight mechanisms

Continued on next page

Table 14.1 – continued from previous page

Stage & Activity	Stakeholder Roles Involved	Governance Focus
Deployment Governance Review (Stage Gate)		
Pre-Deployment Governance Review	Client, project owners, compliance and legal advisors, stakeholder representatives	Confirm readiness for deployment, unresolved risks, accountability assignments, and escalation authority
Usage Stage		
Early-Usage Performance Review	System users, operators, project owners, reference roles	Evaluate operational performance, complaint signals, and stakeholder impacts during early system use
Consequence Stage		
Post-Deployment Monitoring and Review	System users, oversight bodies, project owners, affected stakeholders	Monitor complaints, appeals, disparities, environmental impact, and unintended consequences
Periodic Governance Review	Client, project owners, reference roles, stakeholder representatives	Reassess stakeholder exposure, update governance controls, and adjust escalation mechanisms as risks evolve

14.2 AI Risk and Impact Assessment

Table 14.2: AI Risk and Impact Assessment for governance review and deployment readiness.

Assessment Area	Key Questions	Done
System Purpose and Scope	What decision or process does the AI system support or automate? What organizational objective does the system serve? Are system boundaries and intended use clearly defined?	☐
Stakeholder Exposure	Which stakeholders may be affected during development, usage, or system consequences? Are individuals, communities, workers, or customers exposed to potential harm?	☐
Potential Harms	Could system errors or misuse lead to financial loss, denial of services, privacy violations, discrimination, psychological harm, or environmental impact? Have foreseeable harms been reviewed using the Harm Taxonomy?	☐
Data Risks	Are data sources documented and lawful? Could training data contain bias, representation gaps, or privacy concerns?	☐
Model and System Risks	Could the system produce incorrect, biased, or misleading outputs? Are transparency, explainability, and human oversight requirements defined?	☐
Human Oversight	Are humans able to review, override, or halt system decisions when necessary? Are responsibilities clearly defined for system supervision?	☐
Stakeholder Representation	Are vulnerable or low-influence stakeholders represented through advisors, regulators, or other oversight mechanisms?	☐
Governance Responsibility	Is responsibility assigned for monitoring system impacts and responding to incidents? Are escalation paths defined if harm occurs?	☐
Deployment Readiness	Have identified risks been reviewed and documented? Has the system been approved for deployment under the organization's governance framework?	☐

14.3 Stakeholder Harm Monitoring Dashboard

Table 14.3: Stakeholder Harm Monitoring Dashboard

Stakeholder Group	**Impact Indicator**	**Signal to Monitor**	**Review Frequency**	**Responsible Owner**
Decision subjects	Fairness and access	Appeals, denial rates, error disparities	Monthly / quarterly	Risk or compliance lead
System users	Operational burden	Override rates, complaint patterns, user-reported confusion	Monthly	Operational manager
Workers	Workplace effects	Stress signals, workload changes, productivity or grievance trends	Quarterly	HR / operations
Customers / clients	Service quality and trust	Complaint rates, churn, satisfaction decline	Monthly	Business owner
Communities / public	External impact	Media concerns, public complaints, advocacy alerts	Quarterly / event-driven	Public affairs / governance lead
Environment	Resource impact	Energy use, compute intensity, environmental reporting indicators	Quarterly	Sustainability or technology lead

14.4 Stakeholder Escalation Matrix

Table 14.4: Stakeholder Escalation Matrix

Trigger	Example Situation	Escalation Level	Decision Authority	Required Action
Low-level concern	Minor complaint, isolated usability issue, low-severity error	Operational review	System owner / operational lead	Document issue, review locally, monitor for recurrence
Moderate stake-holder harm	Repeated complaints, unfair outcome pattern, workflow disruption	Project governance review	Project owner / sponsor	Review root cause, assign corrective actions, update controls
High-risk incident	Potential legal breach, severe unfairness, major financial or reputational exposure	Executive escalation	Executive sponsor / governance committee	Pause deployment if needed, initiate formal review, notify oversight functions
Critical impact	Safety risk, rights violation, regulatory breach, widespread stakeholder harm	Crisis escalation	Senior executive / board / legal authority	Stop deployment or use, launch investigation, notify regulators or affected stakeholders

14.5 Governance Decision Log

Table 14.5: Governance Decision Log

Date	Decision	Stakeholders Considered	Risks Reviewed	Decision Authority	Notes / Required Follow-up

Part VII

Closing and References

Stakeholder Excellence in AI Projects

Artificial intelligence systems can create enormous benefits, such as improving healthcare, increasing efficiency, expanding access to services, and supporting better decision-making across many fields.

But the same systems can also cause harm. Automated decisions can affect employment, financial access, public safety, and the integrity of institutions. These impacts may extend beyond the organizations that deploy the technology, affecting individuals, communities, and the environment.

Responsible AI therefore requires more than technical excellence.

It requires attention to the people who may be affected by a system and to the governance structures that guide how systems are designed, deployed, and monitored.

Throughout this book, several key principles have emerged.

- AI systems affect stakeholders across the entire project lifecycle.

- Many of the most affected stakeholders are passive stakeholders who lack direct influence over project decisions.

- Structured stakeholder analysis helps make these risks visible before deployment.

- Governance mechanisms help ensure that responsibility remains clear as systems evolve.

Responsible AI requires several forms of discipline:

- Awareness of who may be affected

- Inclusion of passive stakeholders

- Representation where direct participation is not possible

- Lifecycle-based thinking about system consequences

- Clear accountability for decisions and outcomes

Project teams occupy a unique position in this process. They are often the only group capable of identifying stakeholder risks before systems are deployed and begin influencing real-world decisions.

When stakeholder risks are considered early, projects can incorporate safeguards before harm occurs. When governance structures remain active across the system lifecycle, organizations are better prepared to respond when unexpected consequences appear.

AI innovation and stakeholder responsibility are not opposing goals.

Systems that recognize stakeholder risks are more trustworthy, more resilient, and more sustainable over time.

Responsible AI is therefore not about slowing innovation.

It is about strengthening it, ensuring that technological progress remains aligned with the people and communities it affects.

Appendix A: Sources and Further Reading

This book draws on research from the fields of:

- Artificial Intelligence and Machine Learning
- Project Management
- Stakeholder Theory
- Business Ethics
- Technology Governance
- Data Protection and Privacy Law

Readers interested in deeper academic foundations may explore literature on:

- Stakeholder theory and organizational responsibility
- Algorithmic accountability
- AI ethics frameworks
- Bias and fairness in machine learning
- Sustainable project governance

Appendix B: Emerging AI Frameworks

Governments and professional organizations around the world are developing rules and guidelines for how artificial intelligence should be used. These efforts reflect growing concern that AI systems can affect jobs, financial decisions, privacy, and many other aspects of society.

Several important frameworks are shaping how organizations manage AI responsibly. The following examples illustrate how governments and standards organizations are approaching AI oversight.

NIST AI Risk Management Framework

The United States National Institute of Standards and Technology (NIST) created the AI Risk Management Framework (AI RMF) to help organizations understand and manage the risks associated with artificial intelligence (Tabassi, 2023).

The framework organizes responsible AI practices into three main activities:

- **MAP**: Understand how the AI system works, who may be affected by it, and what risks might arise.
- **MEASURE**: Evaluate how the system performs, including whether it is reliable, fair, and accurate.
- **MANAGE**: Put processes in place to reduce risks and monitor how the system behaves over time.

The framework emphasizes that managing AI risks is an ongoing responsibility. Organizations need to review and monitor their systems throughout the entire technology lifecycle.

ISO/IEC 42001 Artificial Intelligence Management Systems

ISO/IEC 42001 is an international standard that helps organizations manage artificial intelligence in a structured way. Rather than regulating a specific technology, it focuses on how organizations structure their workflow and decision-making around AI (International Standards Organization, 2023).

Organizations that follow ISO 42001 create internal processes for:

- Defining how AI will be used and what goals it should achieve
- Identifying possible risks and impacts
- Putting controls in place to manage those risks

- Reviewing and improving practices over time

The standard follows a continuous improvement cycle common to many management systems: plan, implement, review, and improve. This approach helps organizations treat responsible AI use as an ongoing responsibility rather than a one-time project.

The European Union AI Act

The European Union AI Act is one of the first major laws created specifically to regulate artificial intelligence. It groups AI systems into different risk categories and applies stricter rules to systems that could have significant impacts on people or society (European Union, 2024).

For higher-risk systems, organizations may be required to:

- Document how the system was designed and what data it uses

- Perform checks before the system is put into operation

- Monitor the system's behavior once it is in use

This approach follows the lifecycle of an AI system. Documentation improves transparency during development, pre-deployment checks confirm that the system meets regulatory expectations, and ongoing monitoring helps ensure the system continues to operate responsibly after deployment.

These frameworks differ in scope and legal force, but all emphasize lifecycle governance, documentation, and accountability for AI systems. Organizations should align their internal governance practices with applicable regulatory requirements in their jurisdiction.

Appendix C: Reference Sources for Harms Taxonomy

Table C.1: Harms Taxonomy Reference Sources

Category	Reference
AI System Workers	
Labor Exploitation	(Hao, 2025)
Psychological Harm	(Hao, 2025; Roberts, 2019; Steiger et al., 2021)
Individuals	
Biometric Surveillance Without Consent	(Garvie et al., 2016)
Employment Loss	(Frey & Osborne, 2017)
Financial Loss	(Mittelstadt et al., 2016)
Loss of Freedom / Wrongful Imprisonment	(Buolamwini & Gebru, 2018; Hill, 2020)
Loss of Recourse or Appeal	(Wachter et al., 2016)
Physical Harm	(Russell et al., 2015)
Privacy Loss	(Zuboff, 2019)
Psychological Harm	(Floridi et al., 2018)
Reputational Harm	(Garvie et al., 2016; Hill, 2020)
Wrongful Law Enforcement Interaction	(Garvie et al., 2016)
Organizations	
Algorithmic Opacity	(Mittelstadt et al., 2016)
Financial Loss	(OECD, 2019)
Legal Liability	(Buolamwini & Gebru, 2018)
Operational Harm	(Mittelstadt et al., 2016)
Professional Liability Risk	(Chesney & Citron, 2019)
Reputational Damage	(Floridi et al., 2018)
Strategic Damage	(Mittelstadt et al., 2016)
Local Communities	

Continued on next page

Table C.1 – continued from previous page

Category	Reference
Creative Market Displacement	(Guild, 2023; Samuelson, 2023)
Economic Harm	(Frey & Osborne, 2017; OECD, 2019)
Environmental Damage	(Strubell et al., 2019)
Information Harm	(Tucker et al., 2018)
Institutional Trust Loss	(Floridi et al., 2018)
Loss of Intellectual Property Control	(Samuelson, 2023)
Social Harm	(Garvie et al., 2016)
Society at Large	
Democratic Harm	(Chesney & Citron, 2019)
Economic Inequality	(OECD, 2019)
Environmental Impact	(Patterson et al., 2021)
Institutional Trust Erosion	(Floridi et al., 2018)
Procedural System Disruption	RN1021
Security Risk	(Russell et al., 2015)
Systemic Economic Risk	(OECD, 2019)

End Notes

[1]Kuehnert et al. (2025) examined the development of 224 AI tools and found that developers (78%) and designers (54%) dominated project teams, while organizational leaders appeared in only 18% of cases. End users and affected communities were even less represented, participating in fewer than 11% of the tools studied.

[2]The AI harms taxonomy was developed through a structured review of AI harm literature conducted in March 2026. The literature sources used to construct the taxonomy are provided in the Appendix Table C.1.

[3]These findings draw on an extended version of research conducted between 2023 and 2025 on accountability in AI projects (Miller, 2025). The findings are based on quantitative analysis of survey data from more than 300 respondents across the United States, Germany, China, and South Africa.

Bibliography

Bartz v. Anthropic PBC. (2025, July).

Batchelar v. Interactive Brokers, LLC. (2019).

Buolamwini, J., & Gebru, T. (2018). Gender shades: Intersectional accuracy disparities in commercial gender classification. *Conference on fairness, accountability and transparency*, 77–91.

Chasalow, K., & Levy, K. (2021). Representativeness in statistics, politics, and machine learning. *FAccT '21: Proceedings of the 2021 ACM Conference on Fairness, Accountability, and Transparency, March 310, 2021*, 77–89. https://doi.org/10.1145/3442188.3445872

Chesney, B., & Citron, D. (2019). Deep fakes: A looming challenge for privacy, democracy, and national security. *Calif. L. Rev.*, *107*, 1753.

Davis, K. (2014). Different stakeholder groups and their perceptions of project success. *Int. J. Project Manag.*, *32*(2), 189–201. https://doi.org/10.1016/j.ijproman.2013.02.006

Derry, R. (2012). Reclaiming marginalized stakeholders [Copyright - Springer Science+Business Media Dordrecht 2012 CODEN - JBUEDJ SubjectsTermNotLitGenreText - United States–US]. *J. Bus. Ethics*, *111*(2), 253–264. https://doi.org/10.1007/s10551-012-1205-x

Eskerod, P., & Huemann, M. (2013). Sustainable development and project stakeholder management: What standards say. *Int. J. Manag. Proj. Bus.*, *6*(1), 36–50. https://doi.org/10.1108/17538371311291017

European Commission. (2016). General Data Protection Regulation.

European Union. (2024). Regulation (EU) 2024/1689 of the European Parliament and of the Council of 13 June 2024 laying down harmonised rules on artificial intelligence and amending Regulations (EC) No 300/2008, (EU) No 167/2013, (EU) No 168/2013, (EU) 2018/858, (EU) 2018/1139 and (EU) 2019/2144 and Directives 2014/90/EU, (EU) 2016/797 and (EU) 2020/1828 (Artificial Intelligence Act). http://data.europa.eu/eli/reg/2024/1689/oj

Floridi, L., Cowls, J., Beltrametti, M., Chatila, R., Chazerand, P., Dignum, V., Luetge, C., Madelin, R., Pagallo, U., & Rossi, F. (2018). Ai4peoplean ethical framework for a good ai society: Opportunities, risks, principles, and recommendations. *Minds Mach.*, *28*(4), 689–707.

Frey, C. B., & Osborne, M. A. (2017). The future of employment: How susceptible are jobs to computerisation? *Technol. Forecasting Social Change*, *114*,

254–280. https://doi.org/10.1016/j.techfore.2016.08.019

FTC. (2023). Rite aid banned from using ai facial recognition after ftc says retailer deployed technology without reasonable safeguards. https://www.ftc.gov/

Garvie, C., Bedoya, A., & Frankle, J. (2016). Unregulated police face recognition in america. *Perpetual Line Up.*

Gibert, M., & Martin, D. (2022). In search of the moral status of ai: Why sentience is a strong argument. *AI Soc.*, *37*, 319–330. https://doi.org/10.1007/s00146-021-01179-z

Green, B., & Chen, Y. (2019). Disparate interactions: An algorithm-in-the-loop analysis of fairness in risk assessments. *FAT* '19: Proceedings of the Conference on Fairness, Accountability, and Transparency, January 29-31, 2019*, 90–99. https://doi.org/10.1145/3287560.3287563

Guild, T. A. (2023, March). Authors guild policy proposals regarding the development and use of generative ai.

Hao, K. (2025). *Empire of ai: Inside the reckless race for total domination*. Random House.

Heaton, D., Clos, J., Nichele, E., & Fischer, J. E. (2023). The social impact of decision-making algorithms: Reviewing the influence of agency, responsibility and accountability on trust and blame. *Proceedings of the First International Symposium on Trust-*

worthy Autonomous Systems, Article 11. https://doi.org/10.1145/3597512.3599706

Hill, K. (2020, July). Wrongfully accused by an algorithm.

International Standards Organization. (2023). ISO/IEC 4200 2023-12 information technology — artificial intelligence — management system first edition.

Jones, T. M. (1991). Ethical decision making by individuals in organizations: An issue-contingent model. *Academy of Management Review*, *16*(2), 366–395.

Kuehnert, B., Kim, R., Forlizzi, J., & Heidari, H. (2025). The "who", "what", and "how" of responsible ai governance: A systematic review and meta-analysis of (actor, stage)-specific tools. *Proc. 2025 ACM Conf. Fairness Account. Transpar.*, 2991–3005. https://doi.org/10.1145/3715275.3732191

Martin, K. (2019). Ethical implications and accountability of algorithms. *Journal of Business Ethics*, *160*(4), 835–850. https://doi.org/10.1007/s10551-018-3921-3

Mata v. Avianca, Inc. (2023, June).

Miller, G. J. (2022a). Stakeholder roles in artificial intelligence projects. *Proj. Leadersh. Soc.*, *3, Art. no. 100068*. https://doi.org/10.1016/j.plas.2022.100068

Miller, G. J. (2022b). Stakeholder-accountability model for artificial intelligence projects. *J. Econ. Manag.*, *44*(1), 446–494. https://doi.org/10.22367/jem.2022.44.18

Miller, G. J. (2025). Simultaneous pursuit of accountability for regulatory compliance, financial benefits, and societal impacts in artificial intelligence (ai) projects. *2025 20th Conference on Computer Science and Intelligence Systems (FedCSIS)*, 207–217. https://doi.org/10.15439/2025F6392

Mitchell, R. K., Agle, B. R., & Wood, D. J. (1997). Toward a theory of stakeholder identification and salience: Defining the principle of who and what really counts. *Academy of Management Review*, *22*(4), 853–886. https://doi.org/10.5465/amr.1997.9711022105

Mittelstadt, B. D., Allo, P., Taddeo, M., Wachter, S., & Floridi, L. (2016). The ethics of algorithms: Mapping the debate. *Big Data Soc.*, *3*(2).

Moser, D. C., Hond, P. F. d., & Lindebaum, P. D. (2022). Morality in the age of artificially intelligent algorithms. *Academy of Management Learning & Education*, *21*(1), 139–155. https://doi.org/10.5465/amle.2020.0287

Nisa, U., Shirazi, M., Saip, M. A., & Pozi, M. S. M. (2025). Agentic AI: The age of reasoninga review. *J. Autom. Intell.* https://doi.org/10.1016/j.jai.2025.08.003

OECD. (2019). *Artificial intelligence in society*. https://doi.org/10.1787/eedfee77-en

Patterson, D., Gonzalez, J., Le, Q., Liang, C., Munguia, L.-M., Rothchild, D., So, D., Texier, M., & Dean,

J. (2021). Carbon emissions and large neural network training. *arXiv preprint arXiv:2104.10350.*

Qin, L., Xie, W., & Chen, X. (2025). The impact of knowledge coupling on technological generality in AI: The moderating role of collaborative innovation network centralities. *IEEE Trans. Eng. Manage.*, *72*(4), 2913–2925. https://doi.org/10.1109/TEM.2025.3586481

Roberts, S. T. (2019). *Behind the screen.* Yale University Press.

Russell, S., Dewey, D., & Tegmark, M. (2015). Research priorities for robust and beneficial artificial intelligence. *AI magazine*, *36*(4), 105–114.

Sambasivan, N., Arnesen, E., Hutchinson, B., Doshi, T., & Prabhakaran, V. (2021). Re-imagining algorithmic fairness in india and beyond. *ACM Conference on Fairness, Accountability, and Transparency (ACM FAccT '21), March 310, 2021*, 315–328. https://doi.org/10.1145/3442188.3445896

Samuelson, P. (2023). Legal challenges to generative ai, part i. *Commun. ACM*, *66*(7), 20–23. https://doi.org/10.1145/3597151

Sapkota, R., Roumeliotis, K. I., & Karkee, M. (2026). AI agents vs. agentic AI: A conceptual taxonomy, applications and challenges. *Inf. Fusion, 126, Art. no. 103599.* https://doi.org/10.1016/j.inffus.2025.103599

Steiger, M., Bharucha, T. J., Venkatagiri, S., Riedl, M. J., & Lease, M. (2021). The psychological well-being of content moderators: The emotional labor of commercial moderation and avenues for improving support. *Proceedings of the 2021 CHI conference on human factors in computing systems*, 1–14.

Strubell, E., Ganesh, A., & McCallum, A. (2019). Energy and policy considerations for deep learning in NLP. *arXiv 1906.02243.*

Tabassi, E. (2023, January). Artificial intelligence risk management framework (AI RMF 1.0). https://doi.org/10.6028/NIST.AI.100-1

Tucker, J. A., Guess, A., Barberá, P., Vaccari, C., Siegel, A., Sanovich, S., Stukal, D., & Nyhan, B. (2018). Social media, political polarization, and political disinformation: A review of the scientific literature. *Political polarization, and political disinformation: a review of the scientific literature (March 19, 2018).*

Turner, R. J., & Zolin, R. (2012). Forecasting success on large projects: Developing reliable scales to predict multiple perspectives by multiple stakeholders over multiple time frames. *Proj. Manag. J.*, *43*(5), 87–99. https://doi.org/10.1002/pmj.21289

Wachter, S., Mittelstadt, B., & Floridi, L. (2016). Why a right to explanation of automated decision-making does not exist in the general data protection regulation. *SSRN Electronic Journal.* https://doi.org/10.1093/idpl/ipx005

Walter Auto Loan Tr. v. Track Motors, LLC. (2023, August).

Wieringa, M. (2020). What to account for when accounting for algorithms: A systematic literature review on algorithmic accountability. *FAT* 2020: Proceedings of the 2020 Conference on Fairness, Accountability, and Transparency*, 1–18. https://doi.org/10.1145/3351095.3372833

Zhang, L., Shao, Z., Chen, B., & Benitez, J. (2025). Unraveling generative AI adoption in enterprise digital platforms: The effect of institutional pressures and the moderating role of internal and external environments. *IEEE Trans. Eng. Manage.*, *72*(1), 335–348. https://doi.org/10.1109/TEM.2024.3513773

Zuboff, S. (2019). Surveillance capitalism and the challenge of collective action. *New labor forum*, *28*, 10–29.

Glossary

Accountability The obligation of individuals or organizations to take responsibility for the outcomes of their decisions and actions

Accountability Diffusion A situation where responsibility for decisions or outcomes becomes spread across many individuals or groups, making it unclear who is ultimately responsible

Agentic AI An AI system designed to pursue assigned objectives and carry out sequences of tasks with limited human involvement

AI System Chain The connected sequence of steps—from data collection through model development to real-world decisions—that make up an AI system

Algorithm A step-by-step set of instructions that a computer follows to process data and produce a result or decision

Artificial Intelligence (AI) Computer systems designed to perform tasks that normally require human intelligence, such as learning, reasoning, or decision-making

Bias (Data Bias) Systematic errors in data that cause an AI system to produce unfair or inaccurate results for certain groups

Data Subject A person whose data is collected, stored, or used to train or operate an AI system

Decision Subject A person directly affected by the output of an AI system, such as someone denied a loan or rejected for a job

Decision-Making System An AI system that influences or makes choices that affect individuals, organizations, or society

European Union Artificial Intelligence Act (EU AI Act) A European Union regulation establishing a risk-based legal framework for artificial intelligence systems

Explainability The ability to clearly describe how and why an AI system made a particular decision

Generative AI An AI system that produces new text, images, audio, or other content in response to user prompts, based on patterns learned from large datasets

Governance The framework of rules, roles, and oversight structures that guide how an AI project is managed and controlled

Governance Checkpoint A formal review point in a project where risks, compliance requirements, and ethical considerations are evaluated before the project moves forward

Governance Gap A situation in which responsibility, oversight, or decision authority is unclear or missing in an AI project

Information Asymmetry A situation where one party has more or better information than another, creating risk or imbalance in decision-making

Institutional Accountability Responsibility embedded within organizational rules, roles, and governance systems rather than relying solely on individual judgment

Machine Learning A type of AI where systems learn patterns from data and improve their performance over time without being explicitly programmed for every task

Moral Disengagement A psychological process in which individuals distance themselves from the ethical consequences of their actions

Moral Hazard A risk that occurs when one party takes actions without bearing the full consequences of those actions

NIST AI Risk Management Framework (NIST AI RMF) A voluntary framework developed by the U.S. National Institute of Standards and Technology to help organizations identify and manage AI risks

Passive Stakeholder A person or group who may be harmed by an AI system but has no direct influence over the project that created it

Project Governance The system of leadership, oversight, and control that ensures a project meets its objectives responsibly

Purpose Creep The gradual expansion of how a technology or dataset is used beyond its original purpose without sufficient review or governance

Responsibility Redirection The shifting of responsibility for outcomes to other individuals, teams, or systems rather than accepting direct accountability

Social Drift The gradual normalization of practices that initially appear questionable or risky

Stakeholder Any individual or group that is affected by, or can influence, an AI system or project

Stakeholder Representation The practice of including individuals or groups who can speak on behalf of stakeholders who are unable to directly participate in an AI project

Stakeholder Theory A theory that argues organizations should consider the interests of all affected parties, not just shareholders or paying clients

Structural Accountability Accountability reinforced through formal governance mechanisms such as defined roles, review processes, approval authorities, and documented decision records

Transparency The practice of openly sharing information about how an AI system works, including its limits and risks

Unintended Consequences Outcomes that were not planned or expected when an AI system was designed or deployed

Acronyms

AI Artificial Intelligence

APM Association for Project Management

EU European Union

IEC International Electrotechnical Commission

ISO International Organization for Standardization

NIST National Institute of Standards and Technology

Index

H

I

L

M

N

O

P

R

S

T

U

W

www.ingramcontent.com/pod-product-compliance
Ingram Content Group UK Ltd.
Pitfield, Milton Keynes, MK11 3LW, UK
UKHW061428110926
15101UKWH00046B/142
9 780998 348483